The Epistle of the Eloquent Clarification Concerning the Refutation of Ibn Qutayba

by

Al-Qāḍī al-Nuʿmān b. Muḥammad

(d. 363/974)

Islamic History and Civilization

Studies and Texts

VOLUME 90

The titles published in this series are listed at brill.nl/ihc

The Epistle of the Eloquent Clarification Concerning the Refutation of Ibn Qutayba by Al-Qāḍī al-Nuʿmān b. Muḥammad (d. 363/974)

Critical Edition with an Introduction by

Avraham Hakim

BRILL

LEIDEN · BOSTON
2012

Cover illustration: The third folio of the manuscript of Dhāt al-Bayān (copied 1817–1818) from the Zāhid ʿAlī collection, The Institute of Ismāʿīli Studies, London.

Library of Congress Cataloging-in-Publication Data

Nu'man ibn Muhammad, Abu Hanifah, d. 974.
[Da'a'im al-Islam]
The Epistle of the eloquent clarification concerning the refutation of Ibn Qutayba / al-Qadi al-Nu'man b. Muhammad ; critical edition with an Introduction by Avraham Hakim.
p. cm. — (Islamic history and civilization ; v. 90)
Includes bibliographical references and index.
ISBN 978-90-04-20981-7 (hardback : alk. paper) 1. Islamic law—Early works to 1800. 2. Ismailites—Early works to 1800. 3. Islam—Doctrines—Early works to 1800. 4. Pillars of Islam—Early works to 1800. I. Hakim, Avraham. II. Title.

KBP360.N86A33 2012
340.5'9—dc23

2012007863

This publication has been typeset in the multilingual "Brill" typeface. With over 5,100 characters covering Latin, IPA, Greek, and Cyrillic, this typeface is especially suitable for use in the humanities. For more information, please see www.brill.nl/brill-typeface.

ISSN 0929-2403
ISBN 978 90 04 20981 7 (hardback)
ISBN 978 90 04 21666 2 (e-book)

This book is printed on acid-free paper.

CONTENTS

PREFACE

Al-Qāḍī al-Nuʿmān b. Muḥammad (d. 363/974) began to compose his legal, historical and other literary compilations not long after the foundation of the Fatimid caliphate in North Africa in 296/909. After the Fatimid al-Muʿizz came to power in 341/953, he appointed al-Nuʿmān to the post of supreme judge (*qāḍī-l-quḍāt*), the highest judicial position of the caliphate. It was during this time that al-Nuʿmān compiled his famous *Daʿāʾim al-Islām*, with the guidance of the caliph, as he states. This legal compendium became the founding text of Ismāʿīli jurisprudence.

During this period he also composed the epistle edited here, entitled: "The Epistle of the Eloquent Clarification Concerning the Refutation of Ibn Qutayba". At first glance, this seems to be just one more short legal text, similar to many others he composed. What makes it unique is the fact that in this short compilation the author launches a controversy against Ibn Qutayba (d. 276/889), a highly esteemed Sunni scholar, who lived almost a century earlier.

The controversy pertains both to the role of the jurist as a guide in applying the law and to the source of authority of that law. Ibn Qutayba had claimed in one of his books that the state administrators needed to memorize only some simple legal formulas, transmitted on the authority of the Prophet, his Companions and their disciples, in order to perform their duties efficiently. This, he claimed, would exempt them from the long discussions of the jurists. Al-Nuʿmān composed his epistle to assert that only profound and extensive knowledge of the fine points of the law, transmitted by learned jurists on the authority of the Prophet and the Imāms of his house (*ahl al-Bayt*), could ensure that the officials performed their duties correctly.

This epistle thus is an early Shīʿite refutation of the basic Sunnite doctrines regarding both tradition (*ḥadīth*) and law.

ACKNOWLEDGEMENTS

The edition of this epistle was the result of research on the manuscript epistle of al-Qāḍī al-Nuʿmān, carried out under the auspices and with the subvention of Le Centre National de la Recherche Scientifique (CNRS), Laboratoires d'Etudes sur les Monothéismes, during the summer of 2007.

My thanks are due to members of the Institute of Ismāʿīli Studies (IIS) in London, Professor F. Daftary, Doctor A. Lalani, Mr. Hussein and Mr. Merchant, who graciously made it possible for me to obtain a copy of the manuscript from the Zāhid ʿAlī collection.

Many thanks are due to my friend Ahmad Chleilat from Bourg-la-Reine, France, who drew my attention to the manuscript, put his library at my disposition and shared with me his vast knowledge on Ismāʿīli doctrine and history.

I owe much to my friend and colleague professor M.A. Amir-Moezzi for his assistance and benevolence in the course of my research.

I am indebted to professors Etan Kohlberg, Maribel Fierro and Bruna Soravia for their helpful comments on my work. I extend my deepest gratitude to Professors Wilferd Madelung and Heinz Halm who assisted me in the attempt to identify the addressee of this epistle.

The introduction of the present work is a revised and updated English version of two contributions of mine: the first in French published in two parts in *al-Qanṭara*, vol. XXXI, n. 1 (January–June 2010), pp. 77–102, and vol. XXXI, n. 2 (July–December 2010), pp. 351–369; the second in English published in *Jerusalem Studies in Arabic and Islam* (*JSAI*), n. 38 (2011), pp. 311–336. It was presented at the colloquium "From Jāhiliyya to Islam" in Jerusalem in July 2009.

NOTE TO THE READER

We chose to edit the text of the epistle based on the Zāhid ʿAlī manuscript as our primary text, referred to in the footnotes as الأصل. Following that, we compared the Fyzee manuscript (referred to in the footnotes as ف) with the Zāhid ʿAlī manuscript, and where there were lacunas in the latter they were retrieved them from the Fyzee manuscript within brackets [...]. Furthermore, when the text of the Zāhid ʿAlī manuscript seemed garbled, or when it was obvious that the text of the Fyzee manuscript was more accurate than that of our primary text, we replaced the latter text with that of the former.

The traditions and legal rulings al-Qāḍī al-Nuʿmān quotes on the authority of the Prophet, the *ṣaḥāba* or the Imāms were referred to the earliest Sunnite and Shīʿite sources we could find. Al-Qāḍī al-Nuʿmān's frequent lexical comments were referred to early philological sources, with some of which the author was fairly well acquainted.

We hope to have rendered the final edited text as accurate as its author would have wished to and thus added a new source for the study of Ismāʿīli thought and culture.

INTRODUCTION

1. *The Manuscripts*

This critical and annotated edition of the epistle, *Risālat dhāt al-bayān fī al-radd ʿalā Ibn Qutayba* is based on two manuscripts:

a. *MS 1255—The Zāhid ʿAlī collection*

The Institute of Ismāʿīli Studies in London (IIS) possesses a number of rich manuscript collections. One of these is Doctor Zāhid ʿAlī's (d. 1958) collection, whose MS 1255 contains the epistle edited here. It was misidentified in catalogs of Ismāʿīli manuscripts: It had been reported that only the first half of the work is extant,[1] and that the manuscript contains only the epistle's first eight parts (*juzʾ–ajzāʾ*).[2] In fact, however, the Zāhid ʿAlī manuscript includes all nine parts that constitute the entire work. This is attested by the following quotations:

1) At the end of the ninth part of the epistle (Zāhid ʿAlī) al-Qāḍī al-Nuʿmān states: *fa-hādhā ākhir al-masāʾil allatī dhakarahā Ibn Qutayba*. (This is the last topic mentioned by Ibn Qutayba).
2) At the end of the manuscript, there are the traditional closing formulas signaling the end of the epistle (fols. 88a–88b): *tammat al-risāla bi-ḥamd Allāh wa-ʿawnihi wa-māddat waliyyihi fī arḍihi ʿalayhi asnā taḥiyyātihi wa-salāmihi mā dāma-l-falaku fī maqāmihi.* (The epistle has been concluded with the praise of God and His assistance and [the praise on] the substance of His Favorite on earth [and his assistance], may the best greeting and peace be on Him as long as the firmament remains in its abode). We deemed it necessary to reproduce these final and concluding traditional formulas *in extenso* to demonstrate that the epistle described in the catalogs is indeed complete.

---

[1] Cortese, *Collection*, pp. 156–157 (no. 140); Poonawala, *Biobibliography*, p. 63 (no. 32). See also: Poonawala, "Jurisprudence", note 45. Editors of al-Qāḍī al-Nuʿmān's works usually refer to Poonawala when mentioning our epistle. Note should be taken that this epistle is not listed in the catalog of Ismaili manuscripts compiled by al-Majdūʿ.

[2] Cortese, *Collection*, p. 156.

We shall not give a detailed description of the manuscript here since Cortese has already done so.[3]

b. *The Fyzee Manuscript*

The second manuscript, preserved in the Fyzee collection, comprises 140 folios, with approximately twelve lines per page and is written in a clear *naskhī* hand. It may concluded from the frontispiece and the colophon that initially this manuscript belonged to Ḥusayn b. Nājī Ḥasan Ṣāliḥ Muḥammad al-Yaʿburī al-Qāḍī al-Ḥurayzī al-Yamānī, who sent it (*baʿatha*) at an unidentified date (mentioned in the frontispiece but illegible) to the Ismāʿīlī chief Dāʿī Ṭāhir Sayf al-Dīn b. Muḥammad Burhān al-Dīn (d. 1385/1965). The Fyzee manuscript may also have been copied by the same Ḥusayn b. Nājī.

This manuscript came later to the possession (*dakhala fī mulk*) of professor Asaf Ali Asghar Fyzee (d. 1981) in April 1932 in Bombay, as the eminent Ismāʿīlī scholar mentions in the frontispiece. Fyzee also gave the number 26 to this manuscript.

The Fyzee manuscript includes all nine parts of the epistle. However, part nine was misplaced and located before part eight and its pages numbered accordingly, so that this manuscript actually ends with part eight, followed by the colophon. A careful reading of the manuscript uncovers the confusion, and when part nine is placed in its correct position the manuscript clearly is seen to contain our epistle in its entirety.

2. *The Epistle*

We have chosen to translate the Arabic title *Risālat dhāt al-bayān fī al-radd ʿalā Ibn Qutayba* as "The Epistle of the Eloquent Clarification Concerning the Refutation of Ibn Qutayba, since one of the meanings of *bayān* is "showing of the intent or meaning with the most eloquent expression".[4]

This epistle was known to early[5] and modern biographers of al-Qāḍī al-Nuʿmān, the editors of his works[6] and the catalogers of Ismāʿīli manuscripts.

[3] Cortese, *Collection*, pp. 156–157.

[4] See: Lane, *s.v. b y n.*

[5] Idrīs, *ʿUyūn*, vol. 6, p. 46.

[6] A. A. A. Fyzee made use of a manuscript of our epistle in his edition of al-Qāḍī al-Nuʿmān's *Daʿāʾim al-Islām* and quotes many of its paragraphs in the footnotes of that edition. See al-Qāḍī al-Nuʿmān, *Daʿāʾim*, vol. 2, pp. 27, 32, 43, 72, 83, 87.

One Catalog identifies this epistle as refuting Ibn Qutayba's work *'Uyūn al-ma'ārif*,[7] or as refuting Ibn Qutayba "regarding matters of law (*fiqh*)".[8] The former statement would seem to confuse two different works by Ibn Qutayba, *'Uyūn al-akhbār* and *Kitāb al-ma'ārif*. In fact, neither book is addressed in our epistle, although it does mention the *Kitāb al-ma'ārif*. As for the second assertion, the epistle does not deal with refuting Ibn Qutayba "regarding matters of law" generally. As we learn from reading the beginning of the author's introduction (Zāhid 'Alī, fol. 2a), the epistle aims at treating in detail some legal formulas that Ibn Qutayba listed succinctly in the introduction of his famous work *Adab al-kātib*, a matter which the catalogers neglected to mention altogether.

Furthermore, Lokhandwalla, who published in 1972 an exemplary critical edition of al-Qāḍī al-Nu'mān's *Ikhtilāf uṣūl al-madhāhib*, claims in his introduction that our epistle consists of a refutation of Ibn Qutayba and his son Aḥmad (d. 321/932–933), a famous jurist in his own right who was appointed to the post of judge in Egypt in 321/932–933. Lokhandwalla quotes Ibn Zūlāq (d. 387/997), the famous Egyptian historian and scholar, to the effect that our epistle refutes Ḥanafī jurists. Our reading of *Dhāt al-bayān* does not support any of these claims. As a matter of fact, al-Qāḍī al-Nu'mān refutes all the jurists who disagree with the Imāms of the *ahl al-Bayt*, regardless of their *madhhab* affiliation. Finally, Lokhandwalla states that our epistle survived only until the first half of the sixteen century, and seems to have been unaware of the existence of our two manuscripts.[9]

3. *The Motivation for the Composition of the Epistle*

In his *Adab al-kātib*, Ibn Qutayba claimed that it was enough for a civil servant (*kātib*) to have some basic knowledge of *fiqh* by memorizing a few elementary legal formulas that would exempt him from the long discussions of the jurists.[10] The epistle's introduction makes it clear that al-Qāḍī al-Nu'mān was asked by a high dignitary, who was appointed as tutor to the caliph's sons, to compose a detailed clarification of Ibn Qutayba's succinct list of legal formulas which he mentioned in *Adab al-kātib*. By entitling his epistle *Dhāt al-bayān*, al-Qāḍī al-Nu'man seems to be asserting that, without his detailed clarifications of those succinct formulas, it

[7] Poonawala, *Biobibliography*, p. 63 (no. 32).
[8] Cortese, *Collection*, p. 156.
[9] See: al-Qāḍī al-Nu'mān, *Uṣūl* (ed. Lokhandwalla), "Introduction", p. 42
[10] Ibn Qutayba, *Adab al-kātib*, pp. 13–14.

would not have been possible to apply the law as it should have been. Without his intervention the civil servants would fail their duty, al-Qāḍī al-Nuʿmān seems to caution his reader. It is already in the epistle's title that our author begins the refutation of his opponent.

4. *The Date of the Composition of the Epistle*

The author did not date his composition of the epistle, and as far as we were able to verify he did not mention it in any of his other works. It should be noted that in his *Majālis* al-Qāḍī al-Nuʿmān refutes Ibn Qutayba at length on a point of interpretation of a Qurʾānic verse, but does not mention our epistle.[11] However, the text does contain some internal evidence which may lead us to an approximate date within the frame of al-Qāḍī al-Nuʿmān's entire known output.

More than once, when al-Qāḍī al-Nuʿmān finishes dealing at length with a certain legal point, he refers the reader for further information to the many treatises on *fiqh* he had already composed, stating that some were detailed (*mabsūṭ*) while others were abridged (*mukhtaṣar*).[12] We may thus assume that *Dhāt al-bayān* was not an early work but was composed sometime after al-Qāḍī al-Nuʿmān had finished compiling some of his comprehensive legal works. In this context Poonawala notes that when al-Nuʿmān was appointed to the highest juridical position in the Fatimid state (during al-Muʿizz's reign, 341–365/953–975) he already "had several legal compendia to his credit, in addition to a comprehensive work on Ismāʿīli jurisprudence".[13]

A more specific date can be deduced from another passage in the text, where al-Nuʿmān refers to his famous *Ikhtilāf uṣūl al-madhāhib*.[14] When discussing the various opinions concerning the formula *"al-bayyina ʿalā-l-muddaʿī wa-l-yamīn ʿalā-l-muddaʿā ʿalayhi"* (the proof [is required] from the plaintiff and the oath from the defendant), and the rule that everyone must comply with the Imāms' legal rulings, he comments: *"wa-qad dhakartu mā yūjibu dhālika lahum fī Kitāb uṣūl al-madhāhib wa-gayrihā"* (I have already mentioned what is owed to them [the obedience to the

---

[11] Al-Qāḍī al-Nuʿmān, *Majālis*, pp. 147–152.
[12] See for example: Zāhid ʿAlī, fols. 55a, 58a, 81b, 82a, 86a.
[13] Poonawala, "Jurisprudence", pp. 122–123.
[14] Zāhid ʿAlī, fol. 14b.

Imāms] in the book *Uṣūl al-madhāhib* and in others works). The book's editor, Lokhandwalla, came to the conclusion, based on internal evidence, that the book was composed before 343/954.[15] Thus, it would be possible to deduce that our epistle was composed during al-Muʿizz's reign, an assumption we already introduced above.

Al-Qāḍī al-Nuʿmān refers twice in his text to another work of his, *al-Ikhtilāf wa-l-iftirāq*, which has apparently not survived (except perhaps in a private library).[16] One should note the difference between the author's phrasing in each of these two references. In the first (Zāhid ʿAlī, fol. 38b), as he discusses the various opinions of jurists pertaining to the legal formula *al-zaʿīm ghārim* (the guarantee of a debt is beholden to it), he states: "I will put in writing this and other topics that relate to all the judicial issues in the book *al-Ikhtilāf wa-l-iftirāq*, God willing (*Wa-sawfa uthbitu dhālika wa-ghayrahu mimmā yaʾtī fī abwāb al-futyā kullihā fī Kitāb al-ikhtilāf wa-l-iftirāq in shāʾa Allāh*)".

From this statement we can deduce that al-Qāḍī al-Nuʿmān was preparing to write the book in question, or that he was writing it simultaneously with our epistle. However, at the end of his discussion of the various legal opinions concerning the formula (Zāhid ʿAlī, fols. 55b-57b) *al-bayyiʿān bi-l-khiyār mā lam yaftariqā* (the seller and the buyer have the option [of cancelling the contract] as long as they have not separated), al-Qāḍī al-Nuʿmān writes (Zāhid ʿAlī, fols. 57a–57b): "We have put all this in writing in the book *al-ikhtilāf wa-l-iftirāq* and whoever wishes [more] knowledge on this issue can look in that book and find it there, God willing (*wa-athbatnā dhālika kullahu fī Kitāb al-ikhtilāf wa-l-iftirāq fa-man āthara ʿilm dhālika ṭalabahu fīhi fa-wajadahu in shāʾa Allāh*)". Accordingly, al-Qāḍī al-Nuʿmān may well have completed this book while writing *Dhāt al-bayān*. Be that as it may, these two assertions imply that *al-Ikhtilāf wa-l-iftirāq* was written and probably completed as he was composing our epistle. It seems that this book was a large compilation in which al-Numān indicated where the Sunnite jurists conformed with the Imāms of *ahl al-Bayt* and where they disagreed with them. Later on, he abridged this compilation in a compendium known as *al-muqtaṣar*.[17] Very little is known about these

---

[15] Al-Qāḍī al-Nuʿmān, *Uṣūl* (ed. Lokhandwalla), "Introduction", p. 45. See also: Poonawala "Jurisprudence", p. 139, note 46.

[16] For this book, see: al-Qāḍī al-Nuʿmān, *Uṣūl* (ed. Lokhandwalla), "Introduction", p. 38. See also: Poonawala, "Jurisprudence" p. 139, note 45.

[17] Al-Qāḍī al-Nuʿmān, *Uṣūl* (ed. Lokhandwalla) "Introduction" pp. 38–39. See also, Poonawala, "Jurisprudence", p. 139, note 45.

two works, but with al-Qāḍī al-Nuʿmān's comments in our epistle it may be possible to conclude that they were composed during al-Muʿizz's reign, sometime after 343/954.

5. *Analysis of the Introduction of the Epistle*

Our analysis is based on al-Qāḍī al-Nuʿmān's description of the events that led to the composition of his epistle. We have used the pagination of the Zāhid ʿAlī manuscript.

a. *Fol. 2a: The Tutor and the Fatimid Caliph's Sons*

al-Qāḍī al-Nuʿmān starts by addressing a dignitary whose identity he does not give:

> May God gratify you with His pleasure for your obedience to Him, may He engage you to do His work for His contentment, may He assist you to His satisfaction and that of His Favorite (*walī*, i.e. the caliph) and may He support you in the endeavor he (the caliph) entrusted you with and the post he appointed you to.
>
> You made me bring to you (*aḥḍartanī*), may God grant you success, the book of ʿAbd Allāh b. Muslim b. Qutayba which he composed on the subjects of the correct reading and orthography and declensions (*taqwīm al-lisān wa-l-yad wa-l-iʿrāb*) entitled *Adab al-kuttāb*.[18] You mentioned that you imposed on their highnesses the princes, the sons of the Commander of the Faithful, our lord and master, may God's blessing be on him, to study it owing to the many categories of sciences that it includes. You summed it up for them, simplified its complexities and uncovered what was hidden in it so that they could understand it and learn its content.

We have been unable to identify the addressee of al-Qāḍī al-Nuʿmān's praise at the beginning of the epistle, much as we tried. We understand that this was a high dignitary entrusted to tutor the caliph's sons (al-Muʿizz, if our assumption is correct), who chose to teach them Ibn Qutayba's *Adab al-kātib*. We note al-Qāḍī al-Nuʿmān's expression *aḥḍartanī*, which we rendered as "you made me bring (the book)." The Arabic expression certainly hints at the powerful rank of the addressee who is in a position to "make al-Qāḍī al-Nuʿmān bring a book." We also note the expression: *akhadhta*

[18] Note should be taken that al-Qāḍī al-Nuʿmān used the title *Adab al-kuttāb* and not *Adab al-kātib*. It seems that this title, which was preferred by the scholars of Andalusia, was also common in the Maghreb. See: Soravia, "Préface", p. 542.

al-umarāʾ al-sāda wuld amīr al-muʾminīn, mawlānā wa-sayyidinā ṣalawāt Allāh ʿalayhi bi-ḥifẓihi (you imposed on their highnesses the princes, the sons of the Commander of the Faithful, our lord and master, may God's blessing be on him, to study it). From this expression we may also infer that the addressee of the epistle must have been powerful enough to impose study material on the caliph's sons. He may have been a high-ranking civil servant, a *kātib*, who was entrusted by the caliph to tutor his sons.[19] Many could have been candidates for this post, but with our current knowledge and the fact that we lack additional sources the addressee remains unidentified.

This anonymous tutor thus personally undertook to teach Ibn Qutayba's *Adab al-kātib* to the caliph's sons after he required al-Qāḍī al-Nuʿmān to bring it to him, probably from the Fatimid caliphs' private library. Al-Nuʿmān had an intimate knowledge of this library since he began his duties in the Fatimid administration by collecting and copying books for it.[20] This magnificent library contained a very large number of books, already in the times of the first Fatimid caliphs, and with time became even richer, as our sources attest in detail.[21] In this context one cannot help recalling the episode related by al-Muʿizz, who went to his library searching for a specific book, but once in the presence of such a wealth of books he forgot which one he had come to seek and began reading a number of other books simultaneously; he was so engrossed in reading as he stood there that his feet hurt.[22]

In the above-mentioned text al-Qāḍī al-Nuʿmān relates how the tutor brought to light the contents of *Adab al-kātib* while clarifying its difficulties to his pupils, the princes. In this context it is significant to quote al-Qāḍī al-Nuʿmān's formulation: *fataḥta lahum muqfalahu li-yafhamūhu wa-li-yaʿlamū ʿilma mā fīhi* (you uncovered what was hidden in it so that they could understand it and learn its content). This is the tradition of erudition and teaching held dear by the Fatimids, to which Halm devoted an important study.[23] In this context it is important to note that the Fatimid caliph is the teacher (*muʿallim, muʾaddib*) *par excellence* to his

---

19 In a private communication dated 12/18/07 professor Halm informed me that he had prepared a list of all known Fatimid dignitaries found in written sources, from the beginning of the caliphate (the end of the III/X century) until after al-Mustanṣir's reign (d. 487/1095), but he found no dignitary who held a position of tutor at the Fatimid court.

20 Poonawala, "Jurisprudence", pp. 119–120.

21 Halm, *Learning*, pp. 91–93.

22 Al-Qāḍī al-Nuʿmān, *Majālis*, p. 533, quoted in Halm, *Learning*, p. 91.

23 Halm, *Learning*.

community: on this we refer the reader to Daftary, who speaks of "the doctrine of *taʿlīm*, emphasizing the teaching authority of each Imām independently of his predecessor".[24]

We may well ask why the anonymous tutor chose *Adab al-kātib* as a subject to be taught to the princes. The fact that he selected this work expressly (despite al-Nuʿmān's objection, as we shall point out) demonstrates the importance which he attached to it. This work is indeed a manual, perhaps the first ever written, with the intention to train the *kuttāb*, the civil servants of the state. Ibn Qutayba, who was a *kātib* himself, composed this "manual of the perfect secretary," to borrow Lecomte's expression,[25] in order to rectify the deplorable state of the administration in his time by exposing its inadequacy.[26] Thus, it is possible that the administration of the nascent Fatimid caliphate and its civil service suffered from the same deficiencies as those of the Abbasid caliphate in Ibn Qutayba's time a century before. It will be remembered that we argued above that *Dhāt al-bayān* was composed during al-Muʿizz's reign, and we note here that it was at this time that the Fatimid state finally became stable and began forming its administration. It was indeed al-Muʿizz who "set about endowing the state … with a rigorous administrative and financial organization and solid political and religious institutions" as well as "a clear and homogeneous juridical and doctrinal system."[27] It is likely then that a manual such as *Adab al-kātib* was taught to the princes as a part of their intellectual and practical education as future leaders, taking into account that one of them would be the future caliph, the supreme administrator of the state.

Modern research has shown how well Ibn Qutayba's works were known in Egypt, in the Maghreb and in Andalusia by the end of the third/ninth century and the manner in which they were received in these regions.[28] Indeed they were commonly read and transmitted at the time in the intellectual centers of North Africa, next to the works of Abū ʿUbayd al-Qāsim b. Sallām (d. 224/838) and al-Jāḥiẓ (d. 255/869). We have new evidence that these works were read and discussed in the period preceding the

[24] Daftary, *History and Thought*, "Introduction", p. 6.

[25] Lecomte, "Introduction", p. 46. Modern scholarship owes much to Lecomte's works on Ibn Qutayba and his oeuvre which helped us greatly in this contribution.

[26] Lecomte, *Ibn Qutayba*, pp. 437–443; Lecomte, "Introduction", pp. 46–49.

[27] "al-Muʿizz"; *EI*[2] (F. Dachraoui).

[28] Lecomte, *Ibn Qutayba*, pp. 12–14 et 19–23; Soravia, "Préface", pp. 540–542.

establishment of the Fatimid caliphate, during the conquest of North Africa undertaken by Abū ʿAbd Allāh al-Shīʿī in the name of the Fatimid al-Mahdī.[29] Even then Ibn Qutayba had been already cursed by the Maghreb Shīʿites (*laʿnat Allāh ʿalā Ibn Qutayba*) owing to his anti-Shīʿite views (*ṭaʿnan ʿalā al-Shīʿa*)[30] exactly as he was to be cursed by al-Qāḍī al-Nuʿmān several years later in our epistle, and for the same reason. Some time later, the vizier/secretary Muḥammad b. Aḥmad al-Baghdādī introduced Ibn Qutayba's writings, *Adab al-kātib* included, to the Fatimid court when he came to the Maghreb from the east with the caliph al-Mahdī. It is attested that the high dignitaries at the Fatimid court took pleasure in reading and discussing these works, along with those of al-Jāḥiẓ and other eastern scholars.[31]

Adab al-kātib itself was probably introduced into Egypt by Ibn Qutayba's son, Aḥmad b. ʿAbd Allāh b. Qutayba (d. 322/933) who served there for a short while as judge in 321/932–933.[32] From there this work found its way to North Africa and Andalusia through intermediaries such as the prominent scholar Abū ʿAlī al-Qālī (d. 356/967), to whom it was most likely transmitted by Ibn Qutayba's son Aḥmad.[33] Note should be taken that around the year 329/940, at the early stages of the Fatimid caliphate, al-Qālī stopped for a while in al-Qayrawān on his way to Andalusia, and some his books were lost there.[34] As is well known, al-Qayrawān was a city intimately related to the Fatimids in general and to al-Qāḍī al-Nuʿmān in particular.[35] Owing to the proximity of the times the two men dwelt in al-Qayrawān one wonders whether our author actually met al-Qālī there.

b. *Fols 2a–2b: Al-Qāḍī al-Nuʿmān's Intervention*

Up to this point in his narrative, al-Qāḍī al-Nuʿmān was not called upon to intercede between the tutor and his pupils. However, as a jurist he was

[29] Walker and Madelung, *Advent*, pp. 115–116, referring to Ibn al-Haytham's Arabic text of his *Munāẓarāt* pp. 63, 73.

[30] Walker and Madelung, *id.*, p. 143 referring to Ibn al-Haytham's Arabic text of his *Munāẓarāt*, pp. 94–95.

[31] Halm, *Empire*, pp. 169 et 369.

[32] Lecomte, *Ibn Qutayba*, pp. 13, 19.

[33] Lecomte, *Ibn Qutayba*. pp. 13, 21; Soravia, "Préface", pp. 542–543.

[34] "Al-Ḳālī", *EI²* (Sellheim).

[35] Al-Qāḍī al-Nuʿmān studied in Qayrawān at the beginning of the Fatimid insurrection and ended up being appointed as judge of that city by the caliph al-Manṣūr in 337/948. See: "al-Nuʿmān", *EI²* (Dachraoui); Hamdani, *Revolution*, pp. 46–47.

asked by the tutor to assist him to clarify certain legal issues mentioned in *Adab al-kātib*:

> You approached a chapter of this book that deals with certain formulas pertaining to legal matters. You required from me to explain them to you so that it would be possible for you to clarify these issues to them (i.e. the princes), among other issues that you explained and established by your own knowledge. You read that chapter before me (*qara'ta 'alayya*) and I answered your questions explaining its contents and its problems. I indicated to you what was reliable in it and what was not. Then you requested from me to put all this in writing in a book with ample details (*basṭ*) in order to better confirm the learning, better clarify the evidence and keep it safer from additions and lacunas. Thus, I was of the opinion of putting in writing a book with ample details, as you requested, so that the princes could better benefit from the knowledge it includes....

Al-Qāḍī al-Nuʿmān was thus required, in his capacity as a jurist, to clarify a paragraph from *Adab al-kātib* which included the legal formulas mentioned by its author. At first this clarification was performed orally, by which we deduce that the tutor was not a specialist in legal matters. Note should be taken of the expression *qaràta 'alayya* "you read before me" by which we understand that in legal matters al-Qāḍī al-Nuʿmān became the teacher who explained the legal points to the tutor. The latter was not satisfied and asked the jurist to put his explanations in a book with ample details (*basaṭa*), which brought about the composition of our epistle. This may point to al-Qāḍī al-Nuʿmān's position as the highest legal authority in the empire, a position he reached at the time of al-Muʿizz.

c. *Fols. 2b–3b Ibn Qutayba's Legal Formulas*

Here al-Qāḍī al-Nuʿmān quotes all the legal formulas which Ibn Qutayba mentioned in his introduction of *Adab al-kātib*, one-by-one.[36] Our author declared that he intended to discuss them all and refute his opponent's views on each by means of lengthy legal arguments. This was presumably the main reason for the epistle's composition. In fact al-Qāḍī al-Nuʿmān refuted all Sunni views that did not agree with those of the *ahl al-Bayt*.

---

[36] A comparison between the texts of *Adab al-kātib* and our epistle shows that al-Qāḍī al-Nuʿmān quoted Ibn Qutayba to the letter, apart from some insignificant differences that may have been the result of copyists' errors.

d. *Fols. 3b–4b Al-Qāḍī al-Nuʿmān's Arguments against his Opponent*

al-Qāḍī al-Nuʿmān then devotes a long chapter exposing his claims against his antagonist. The chapter is entitled *dhikr ighfāl Ibn Qutayba fīmā basaṭahu qabl hādhā al-faṣl mimmā dhakara annahu yanbaghī li-ṭālib al-ʿilm an yaʿlamahu wa-yaʾkhudha bihi nafsahu* (Ibn Qutayba's negligence in what he wrote in detail in the previous chapter, pertaining to the sciences the scholar has to acquire and put into practice).

> Know, may God watch over you, that even though scholars of the Arabic language (*ahl al-ʿilm bi-l-lisān*) consider Ibn Qutayba to be trustworthy regarding both the knowledge he transmitted from the early scholars as well as the careful composition of the material he collected and studied, he is still one of the enemies of God and His Favorites, the opponent and the fierce detractor of the truth and of those who hold it. This is a scholar of little worth (*ḥashwī*) belonging to the common people (or: a Sunnite, *ʿāmmī*) who believes in anthropomorphism (*tashbīh*), rejects the imamate of the family of the Prophet, may the praise of God be on him and on his Family, and supports the imamate of their enemies so much that he surpasses the majority of the Sunnites on this issue. He even mentioned al-Ḥusayn b. ʿAlī, may the praise of God be on him, in his book *Kitāb al-maʿārif*, saying: "As for Ḥusayn he was known as Abū ʿAbd Allāh. He rebelled against Yazīd; therefore ʿUbayd Allāh b. Ziyād sent ʿUmar b. Saʿd b. Abī Waqqāṣ[37] to fight him. As a result Sinān b. Qays al-Nakhaʿī[38] killed him". Thus the enemy of God Ibn Qutayba categorized Ḥusayn among the rebels (*khawārij*) and the cursed Yazīd son of the cursed Muʿāwiya among the imāms. This is his belief and the belief of those of share his views, as it was reported that Mālik [b. Anas] had said: *mā kuntu uḥibbu li-ʿAlī al-khurūj ʿalā Muʿāwiya* (I would have preferred that ʿAlī did not rebel [or: set out to fight] against Muʿāwiya).[39] Had I not feared that this book (i.e. the epistle) goes beyond what I intended in the first place, I would have quoted the terms of contempt and aggression that Ibn Qutayba uttered against the Imāms from the Prophet's family and against their faithful supporters. No one believes that his reports are truthful when they pertain to God's religion and commandments and to what God made lawful or prohibited, and [no one believes] that he is trustworthy or that one may learn anything from him.

al-Qāḍī al-Nuʿmān does mention Ibn Qutayba's prominence as a serious scholar in the field of secular knowledge, basically in the realm of the

[37] The two manuscripts we used read: ʿAmr b. Saʿd, which seems to be a scribal error.

[38] See for this name the comments below.

[39] Note should be taken that in the Zāhid ʿAlī manuscript the expression *li-ʿAlī* was glossed in a different handwriting after the term *al khurūj*. However, this expression is well attested in the text in F. We shall comment on this gloss hereafter.

Arabic language, thus conceding that his opponent did indeed enjoy a high reputation among eastern and western scholars at this period. However, he challenges him in the realm of religious *ʿilm*. When he describes Ibn Qutayba as *ḥashwī*, he means to say his opponent is an unreliable scholar who transmits the traditions, the *ḥadīth*, from untrustworthy sources. Al-Qāḍī al-Nuʿmān believes that the transmission of traditions should be undertaken by scholars of his own kind, who believe that trustworthy *ḥadīth* should be quoted solely on the authority of the holy Imāms of *ahl al*-Bayt. Al-Nuʿmān couples the accusation of *ḥashwiyya* with that of anthropomorphism (*tashbīh*),[40] an accusation brought against Ibn Qutayba by some Sunnite scholars as well.[41]

When he accuses Ibn Qutayba of being *ʿaduww min aʿdāʾ Allāh wa-aʿdāʾ awliyāʾhi* (one of the enemies of God and His Favorites), it seems that he is alluding to his opponent's harsh criticism of the political claims of the extremist Shīʿites (*ghulāt, rāfiḍa*) and his sharp condemnation of the *bāṭiniyya* who based their doctrines on an esoteric interpretation of the Qurāʾn.[42] Al-Qāḍī al-Nuʿmān must have been aware of Ibn Qutayba's real attitude towards non-extremist Shīʿites: Ibn Qutayba does not condemn a moderate veneration of ʿAlī but does not admit the latter's supposed infallibility or his preeminence over other companions of Muḥammad, especially the first three Rightly Guided caliphs.[43]

Al-Qāḍī al-Nuʿmān's quotation from Ibn Qutayba's *Kitāb al-maʿārif* is perplexing, to say the least. Here we have juxtaposed the text quoted in *Dhāt al-bayān* and the corresponding text from *Kitāb al-maʿārif* as it had reached us:

---

[40] See: Lecomte, *Ibn Qutayba*, pp. 336–337; see also: *ḥas̲h̲wiyya*, *EI*[2]. Several scholars associated the *ḥashwiyya* with the anthropomorphists (*mujassima*). See: Ibn ʿAsākir, *Tabyīn*, pp. 149–151; see also: Shahrastānī, *Milal*, vol. 1, p. 105: "Some *ḥashwiyya* (unreliable) scholars clearly declared their belief in *tashbīh*" (*ṣarraḥū bi al-tashbīh*)".

[41] Lecomte, *Ibn Qutayba*, pp. 328–329. See: Dhahabī, *Siyar*, vol. 13, pp. 298–299 where Ibn Qutayba is also accused of being a *karrāmite*. See: "Karrāmiyya", *EI*[2] (Bosworth).

[42] Lecomte, *Ibn Qutayba*, pp. 309– 314; Lecomte, *divergences*, pp. 79–82.

[43] Lecomte, *Ibn Qutayba*, pp. 315–317.

Dhāt al-Bayān	*Kitāb al-maʿārif*
As for Ḥusayn he was known as Abū ʿAbd Allāh. **He rebelled against Yazīd *(kharaja ʿalā Yazīd)*** and therefore ʿUbayd Allāh b. Ziyād sent ʿUmar b. Saʿd b. Abī Waqqāṣ to fight him. As a result Sinān b. Qays al-Nakhaʿī killed him.[44]	As for al-Ḥusayn b. ʿAlī b. Abī Ṭālib he was known as Abū ʿAbd Allāh. **He departed (i.e. from Medina) intending to reach al-Kūfa *(kharaja yurīd al-Kūfa)*** and ʿUbayd Allāh b. Ziyād sent ʿUmar b. Saʿd b. Abī Waqqāṣ against him. As a result Sinān b. Abī Anas al-Nakhaʿī killed him.[45]

One can attribute the faulty name of al-Ḥusayn's murderer in both manuscripts of *Dhāt al-bayān* to a mistake of an earlier copyist, for we believe that the very erudite al-Qāḍī al-Nuʿmān could not have been ignorant of the name of Sinān b. Abī Anas al-Nakhaʿī and would not have mistakenly replaced it with that of the anonymous Sinān b. Qays al-Nakhaʿī (unless the *kunya* of Qays, Sinān's father, was Abū Anas, which we did not find in the sources). More problematic is the divergence between Ibn Qutayba's expression *kharaja yurīd al-Kūfa* (he departed intending to reach al-Kūfa) and al-Qāḍī al-Nuʿmān's *kharaja ʿalā Yazīd* (he rebelled against Yazīd). Even if we admit that the term *yurīd* in Arabic may be read as *Yazīd* (a simple dot on the "r" would turn it into a "z") it is still hard to explain the addition of the preposition *ʿalā* in *Dhāt al-bayān*, which profoundly alters the meaning of the whole expression, and the enigmatic absence in our epistle of the word *al-Kūfa* attested in Ibn Qutayba's text.

Kitāb al-maʿārif was a well-known work and it is hardly credible that al-Qāḍī al-Nuʿmān, his great prestige notwithstanding, would have altered the original text intentionally just to substantiate his attacks against his opponent and confirm the latter's animosity towards the *ahl al-Bayt*. One plausible explanation for this divergence is that al-Qāḍī al-Nuʿmān had at his disposal a different version of *al-Maʿārif* than the one that has come down to us. Indeed, the text of this book was reshaped many times since it was conceived as a "history handbook to which several appendixes were adduced from time to time."[46] It may be that an earlier version than the one in our possession contained the text as al-Qāḍī al-Nuʿmān quoted it. The modern editor of the book, notes no divergences pertaining to the

[44] Al-Qāḍī al-Nuʿmān, *Dhāt al-bayān*, Zāhid ʿAlī, fol. 4a.
[45] Ibn Qutayba, *Maʿārif*, p. 213.
[46] Lecomte, *Ibn Qutayba*, p. 125.

text quoted above among the various manuscripts on which he based his edition.[47]

Next al-Qāḍī al-Nuʿmān strove to demonstrate that his opponent was not the only Sunnite scholar who considered the Imāms of the Prophet's family as rebels and their enemies as legitimate rulers. He quotes Mālik b. Anas (d. 179/795) who is reported to have disapproved of rebellion against Muʿāwiya (*mā kuntu uḥibbu al-khurūj ʿalā Muʿāwiya*), as we have seen above. In the Zāhid ʿAlī manuscript the expression *li-ʿAlī* was glossed after the verb *uḥibbu*, rendering Mālik's utterance as *mā kuntu uḥibbu li-ʿAlī al-khurūj ʿalā Muʿāwiya* (I would have preferred that ʿAlī did not rebel against Muʿāwiya). Yet it should be noted that the expression *li-ʿAlī* is attested after the verb *uḥibbu* in the text of the Fyzee manuscript. Be that as it may, we did not find either of these two utterances in the sources we checked. But another utterance expressing disapproval of ʿAlī's policy pertaining to the Battle of the Camel is indeed attributed to Mālik; the latter was asked about the legality of ʿAlī's departure [i.e. from Medina to wage war against his enemies in Iraq], and ruled: *kāna khurūj ʿAlī khaṭaʾan* (ʿAlī's departure was a mistake).[48] It is plausible therefore that al-Qāḍī al-Nuʿmān quoted the above utterance attributed to Mālik from some lost source and did not make it up. Further evidence for this can be deduced from the Mālikite scholarly milieu in the Maghreb at the eve of the Fatimid conquest. These scholars were overtly pro-Umayyad and expressed opinions that were clearly in line with the above-quoted expression attributed by al-Qāḍī al-Nuʿmān to Mālik. A new source attests that two of them were executed for having affirmed "the pre-eminence of Muʿāwiya over the lord of all people" (i.e. ʿAlī) (*faḍl Muʿāwiya ʿalā sayyid al-bashar*)[49] and that "ʿAlī had no legal right to claim the imamate and should not, therefore, have waged war against Muʿāwiya".[50]

This indicates that the gist of the statement attributed to Mālik by al-Qāḍī al-Nuʿmān was taken up later by pro-Umayyad Mālikite scholars

[47] See: Ibn Qutayba, *Maʿārif*, Introduction, pp. 82–100.

[48] Ibn Ḥabīb, *Taʾrīkh*, p. 115.

[49] Generally it is the Prophet who is called *sayyid al-bashar*, "the lord of all people". However, some Shīʿite traditions attribute this title to ʿAlī. See: Mufīd, *Tafḍīl*, p. 35 (the companion Jābir b. ʿAbd Allāh is supposed to have said: "ʿAlī is the lord of all people and only an unbeliever would doubt it". (*ʿAlī sayyid al-bashar lā yashukku fīhi illā kāfir*). See also: Idrīs, *ʿUyūn*, vol. 6, pp. 288–292, where the author argues at length for the legitimacy of calling ʿAlī "the best of the people" (*khayr al-bashar*).

[50] Walker and Madelung, *Advent*, p. 30, referring to ʿIbn al-Haytham's Arabic text of his *Munāẓarāt* p. 118.

who believed that Muʿāwiya was the legitimate caliph while ʿAlī was to be considered the rebel. Consequently, it may be assumed that al-Qāḍī al-Nuʿmān did not falsely attribute this expression to Mālik and quoted it from some unknown source. By pointing out to this link between the expressions of Ibn Qutayba and Mālik, our author further demonstrates his opponent's animosity to the *ahl al-Bayt*.

Al-Qāḍī al-Nuʿmān's last comment in this section, "[no one believes] that he, i.e. Ibn Qutayba, is trustworthy or that one may learn anything from him" may have been addressed to the anonymous tutor, and reflects our author's objection to choosing *Adab al-kātib* as teaching material for the princes.

e. *Fols. 4b–7a: The Importance of the Jurists' Discussions*

Al-Qāḍī al-Nuʿmān finally approaches the issue which matters the most to him, and which probably motivated the composition of the epistle: the duty of the jurist, the *faqīh*, as the interpreter of the law. In his opinion Ibn Qutayba advised civil servants to ignore the long discussions of the *fuqahāʾ* on law. And thus he wrote:

> Ibn Qutayba affirmed: "he (the civil servant) needs to acquire a theoretical knowledge of the principles of *fiqh* and a technical knowledge of the basics (*uṣūl*) of the tradition of the Messenger of God and his Companions. Then he mentioned these formulas which we quoted above after having urged the civil servants to know and study several other sciences. Pertaining to the sciences of *fiqh* he restricted himself to the knowledge of the formulas he mentioned, pretending that this will exempt the civil servants "from the long discussions of the jurists" (*iṭālat al-fuqahāʾ*). His words reflect his ignorance in matters of *fiqh*, his lack of desire to be involved with it and his abstaining from it. It would have been better for him to put *fiqh* at the head of the list of the sciences he urged the civil servants to know, and to enjoin them to study what God requires from the believers to know, in order to be able to apply the laws that His religion imposes on them. Instead, he restricted them to the knowledge of these short legal formulas, pretending that these will exempt them from the need to know other formulas. After the affirmation of the Unity of God and the recognition of His favorites by whom the acts of devotions of the believers are accepted, he should have urged the civil servants to know the duties of purification, prayer, alms, fasting, pilgrimage and *jihād* because these are the pillars on which Islam is founded (*daʿāʾim al-Islām allatī buniya ʿalayhā*).

What provoked al-Qāḍī al-Nuʿmān's strong resentment was mainly his opponent's assertion that the mere knowledge of short legal formulas was enough for civil servants and exempted them from gaining familiarity with the jurists' long discussions on law. Al-Qāḍī al-Nuʿmān firmly believed that these discussions were precisely what the *kuttāb* needed most in order to be able to apply God's law correctly. In fact, it was clear that Ibn Qutayba's assertion rendered the function of the *faqīh* superfluous. If our assumption is correct and *Dhāt al-bayān* was indeed composed during al-Muʿizz's reign, al-Qāḍī al-Nuʿmān was at that time the most important jurist and the most prolific author of works on legal matters in the Fatimid realm. It is reasonable, then, that he would refute Ibn Qutayba on a point that would have rendered his life's work superfluous. He certainly did not wish to have the Fatimid princes learn from Ibn Qutayba's assertion that they could do without a *faqīh* to guide them when it came to the application of the law.

Al-Qāḍī al-Nuʿmān takes the opportunity to focus in this section of his introduction on a subject dear to his heart, "the seven pillars of Islam," on which he based the composition of his famous juridical compendium, *Daʿāʾim al-Islām*.[51] This compendium was in fact compiled during the reign, and with the guidance, of al-Muʿizz[52] and therefore if it had been composed prior to *Dhāt al-bayān*, it can be assumed that al-Qāḍī al-Nuʿmān would quite likely have mentioned it in this section of the epistle.

Next our jurist discusses at length the need to acquire knowledge (*ʿilm*) and affirms that the long discussions of the jurists amount to indispensable *ʿilm*. He quotes the known Prophetical tradition according to which each Muslim, man or woman, is required to seek knowledge (*ṭalab al-ʿilm*). Then he deals with the duties of prayer, purification and fasting, insisting that these should be taught to children even by force. To prove these propositions he refers to traditions transmitted on the authority of the Prophet, ʿAlī, al-Bāqir and al-Ṣādiq. Following this al-Qāḍī al-Nuʿmān challenges Ibn Qutayba's assertion again, saying:

> The long discussions of the *fuqahāʾ* are all knowledge (*taṭwīl al-fuqahāʾ ʿilm kulluhu*) and anyone who pretends to avoid them does not know the value of knowledge and ignores knowledge itself. What a shame for one who seems to know these formulas mentioned by Ibn Qutayba, who pretends that they exempt him from further knowledge, but when he performs the purification [with water] or washes himself or performs the purification by dust, *tayammum*, it becomes evident that he does not know how to performs these duties. Similarly he needs to pray but does not know how, or when he is asked about his religion he does not know what to answer.

---

[51] For the "Seven Pillars of Islam", see: Halm, *Empire*, pp. 370–374.

[52] Halm, *op. cit.* p. 371.

al-Qāḍī al-Nuʿmān goes on to quote a singular episode: while the Muslims were on their way to a campaign (*ghazwa*) the Prophet was informed that ʿAmmār b. Yāsir has been seen rolling naked in the sand (*yatamaʿʿak ʿuryān fī al-turāb*). Muḥammad asked ʿAmmār why was he rolling in the sand like a donkey would (*kamā yatamaʿʿak al-ḥimār*) and ʿAmmār answered that he wanted to perform *tayammum* because he had no water for purification. Muḥammad started laughing and taught ʿAmmār how to perform *tayammum* correctly.[53] Al-Qāḍī al-Nuʿmān comments that all ʿAmmār needed was to consult the Qurʾān on this matter.[54] Then our author continues to refute Ibn Qutayba:

> Likewise, the leaders (*aʾimma*) whose examples the ignorant Ibn Qutayba follows were mistaken, pertaining to a large number of juridical matters and rendered many erroneous judgments on what is lawful or unlawful (*al-ḥalāl wa-l-ḥarām*); the same is true for his disciples who profess his doctrine and to many others who did not pay heed to the knowledge of jurisprudence and confined themselves to the knowledge he urged them to acquire, pretending that they did not need more. As for example Abū Bakr, who ordered to cut off the hand of a guest who had stolen whereas it is known that cutting the hand of such a guest is unlawful; or ʿUmar, who ordered to lapidate a pregnant women convicted of fornication while such a pregnant woman should not be lapidated until she had given birth to her child.[55] There are many examples like these which we cannot mention here because they go beyond the framework of our book. Such examples are transmitted about these people and we have witnessed in our days similar examples concerning many contemporary illustrious [disciples] of Ibn Qutayba.

f. *Fols. 7a–8b: The Refutation of Contemporary Mālikite Scholars*

Al-Qāḍī al-Nuʿmān affirms that it is not necessary to mention examples of the ignorance of contemporary Mālikite scholars who, in accordance with Ibn Qutayba's assertion, knew nothing about the fine points of the law and were satisfied with a few legal formulas they knew by heart. Yet despite his claim, it seems that he could not refrain from the temptation to ridicule them and expose their ignorance in the application of the law,

---

[53] We could not find this episode exactly as quoted by al-Qāḍī al-Nuʿmān in the sources we consulted whether Sunnite or Shīʿite. For a different version that includes the gist of the story, see. Ṭabarānī, *Awsaṭ*, vol. 2, p. 13.

[54] al-Qāḍī al-Nuʿmān is referring to the verse 4:43 according to which: "...and if you can find no water, have recourse to wholesome dust and wipe your faces and your hands".

[55] For similar reports, see: Ibn Shādhān, *Īḍāḥ*, p. 195.

especially because the Mālikites were always opposed to the Fatimid occupation of North Africa.

He relates that Abū ʿAbd Allāh al-Shīʿī, the grand master of Fatimid propaganda in the Maghreb (*ṣāḥib al-daʿwa fī-l-Maghrib*), met a Mālikite judge in al-Qayrawān and asked him what reference he used when applying the law; the jurist affirmed that he referred to the Sunna. Abū ʿAbd Allāh asked him to explain what the Sunna meant and the Mālikite answered: "The Qurʾān is the word of God uncreated" (*al-Qurʾān kalām Allāh ghayr makhlūq*). Al-Qāḍī al-Nuʿmān commented that this jurist was ridiculed by everyone present. We did not find this episode in the sources we consulted. However, the debates between Abū ʿAbd Allāh and the Mālikites on dogma in general and on the Sunna in particular, and precisely in al-Qayrawān, are well attested in the sources.[56]

Note should be taken that, even if it was ridiculed by al-Qāḍī al-Nuʿmān, the Mālikite judge's answer was not totally inappropriate. It reflected the controversy between Mālikites and pro-Muʿtazilite Ḥanafites in late third/ninth-century Qayrawān on the issue of "the creation of the Qurʾān" (*khalq al-Qurʾān*). The pro-Muʿtazilite Ḥanafites, who supported the Fatimids, were of the opinion that the Qurʾān was created (*al-Qurʾān makhlūq*), whereas the Mālikites sided with the majority of Sunnis and professed that it was "the uncreated Word of God."[57] Consequently, it stands to reason that when asked about the Sunna the Mālikite judge referred to what the Sunna meant for him.

Al-Qāḍī al-Nuʿmān, next, reports on another Mālikite jurist who criticized Ḥanafite jurists (*al-ʿIrāqiyyūn*)[58] in al-Qayrawān. It was well known that this jurist had a very poor knowledge of the law. He was asked how much a man who had made a profit of two hundred dirham had to pay as alms. After some thinking the Mālikite replied that he should give two dirham as charity. He, too, was ridiculed and told bluntly that his ignorance regarding alms should have prevented him from criticizing other jurists.

Al-Nuʿmān then brings the story of a third Mālikite scholar who was appointed as judge by a certain *qāḍī* (*istaḥkamahu baʿḍ al-quḍāt*). One day the latter asked his new appointee to tell him of a case brought before him and the sentence he rendered. The new appointee replied that he rendered a verdict against a missing person (*ghāʾib*). The judge praised

[56] Halm, *Empire*, pp. 240–247.

[57] On this controversy at that time in Qayrawān, see: Madelung and Walker, *Advent*, pp. 20–23.

[58] For this reference to Ḥanafites as "Iraqis", see: Madelung and Walker, *Advent*, p. 21.

him, saying that his verdict was in conformity with the Sunna. Then he asked him where the missing person was located, and he replied that he was about two miles away (*qadr mīlayn*). The judge exclaimed: "Woe to you, you put us all to shame. You cannot render such a verdict against someone who is located so near".

Finally, al-Qāḍī al-Nuʿmān gives another example to illustrate the negative consequences of ignorance of the finer points of the law. He relates that a dignitary of the Prophet's family (*baʿḍ aṣḥāb al-nasab al-sharīf*) was given the honor of publicly reciting the prayer of the dead near the grave of a deceased person. The dignitary could not refuse, but did not know how to perform that prayer. So he recited the regular prayer, which put him to ridicule. A better-informed scholar came to the rescue and recited the prayer for the dead according to custom.

Al-Qāḍī al-Nuʿmān concludes his introduction as follows:

> Indeed the first knowledge one has to acquire is to comprehend what is crucial in the realm of *fiqh* and what is necessary in order to perform the acts of devotion. After this, every other knowledge one acquires only enriches and honors him more. God said (Qurʾān 58:11): "God will raise up in rank those of you who believe and have been given knowledge". He also said (Qurʾān 39:9): "Are they equal those who know and those who know not? Only men possessed of minds remember". And ʿAlī, praise of God be on him, said: "the value of a person is inherent in what he knows well" (*qīmatu kulli-imriʾin mā kāna yuḥsinu*).[59]

6. *Conclusion: The Total Refutation of Ibn Qutayba and His* Adab al-Kātib

The impression given by the epistle's introduction, and the epistle as a whole, is that al-Qāḍī al-Nuʿmān criticized Ibn Qutayba for three main reasons:

a) Ibn Qutayba's fame: as a scholar his works were widely acknowledged in the east as well as in the west of the Islamic world. His work *Adab al-kātib* was considered as the primary handbook for educating civil servants.
b) Ibn Qutayba's refutation of the extremist Shīʿites, and especially the *Bāṭiniyya*.

[59] See: Majlisī, *Biḥār*, vol. 4, pp. 165–166.

c) Above everything else, Ibn Qutayba's assertion that civil servants should limit their knowledge of the law to a number of memorized legal formulas, and that consequently they could do without the lengthy explanations of the jurists. This assertion al-Qāḍī al-Nu'mān could not pass over. He may well have considered the fact that *Adab al-kātib* was chosen as study material for the princes, one of whom would rule the Fatimid state in the future, as a real threat to the position of the *faqīh* in the state hierarchy.

In this context it should be noted that al-Qāḍī al-Nu'mān considered *Adab al-kātib*, probably because of its fame throughout the Muslim world at that time, to be a dangerous compendium that causes more harm than good. Although not mentioned in the epistle's introduction, his negation of that book is included in a paragraph of the epistle where he confronts Ibn Qutayba once more, regarding the "long discussions of the jurists". Al-Qāḍī al-Nu'mān writes (Zāhid 'Alī, fol. 71a):

> He (Ibn Qutayba) did not restrict the knowledge he transmitted in that book (*Adab al-kātib*), where he emphasized his declaration [regarding the long discussions of the jurists], to the religious sciences only, but he deeply immersed himself in it in many secular sciences (*al-'ulūm al-dunyawiyya*), so much that he exceeded what should have been enough for the addressees of such detailed knowledge (i.e. the *kuttāb*). Yet, he classified [religious] knowledge and aimed intentionally at what was needed to be studied and known, which he was compelled to do, but he erased it completely and restricted it to [the succinct legal formulas], forsaking thus the knowledge, rejecting it and abstaining from it.

Following his introduction, al-Qāḍī al-Nu'mān discusses at length each one of the legal formulas mentioned by Ibn Qutayba in the introduction of his *Adab al-kātib*.

ABBREVIATIONS AND BIBLIOGRAPHY

Primary Sources

Ibn Abī al-Ḥadīd, *Sharḥ* = Ibn Abī al-Ḥadīd, ʿAbd al-Raḥmān. *Sharḥ nahj al-balāgha*. Ed. Muḥammad Abū-l-Faḍl Ibrāhīm. Beirut, 1987.

Ibn Abī Shayba, *Muṣannaf* = Ibn Abī Shayba, ʿAbd Allāh b. Muḥammad. *Al- Muṣannaf fī-l-aḥādīth wa-l-āthār*. Ed. Saʿīd al-Laḥḥām. Beirut, 1989.

Ibn ʿAsākir, *Tabyīn* = Ibn ʿAsākir, ʿAlī b. Al-Ḥasan. *Tabyīn kadhib al-muftarī fī mā nusiba ilā al-imām Abī al-Ḥasan al-Ashʿarī*. Beirut, 1404 (AH).

Ibn Ḥabīb, *Taʾrīkh* = Ibn Ḥabīb, ʿAbd al-Malik. *Kitāb al-taʾrīkh*. Ed. Jorge Aguadé. Madrid, 1991.

Ibn Qutayba, *Adab al-kātib* = Ibn Qutayba, ʿAbd Allāh b. Muslim. *Adab al-kātib*. Ed. Muḥammad al-Dālī. Beirut, 1986.

—— *Maʿārif* = Ibn Qutayba, ʿAbd Allāh b. Muslim. *Al-Maʿārif*. Ed. Tharwat ʿUkāsha. Cairo, n.d.

Ibn Manẓūr, *Lisān* = Ibn Manẓūr, Muḥammad b. Mukarram. *Lisān al-ʿArab*. Cairo, n.d.

Idrīs, *ʿUyūn* = Idrīs ʿImād al-Dīn. *ʿUyūn al-akhbār wa-funūn al-āthār*. Ed. Muṣṭafā Ghālib. Beirut, 1996.

Majdūʿ = Al-Majdūʿ, Ismāʿīl b. ʿAbd al-Rasūl. *Fihrist al-kutub wa-l-rasāʾil wa-li-man hiya min al-ʿulamāʾ*. Ed. ʿAlī Naqī Manzawī. Tehran, 1966.

Majlisī, *Biḥār* = Al-Majlisī, Muḥammad Bāqir. *Biḥār al-anwār al-jāmiʿa li-durar akhbār al-aʾimma al-aṭhār*. Beirut, 1983.

Mālik, *Muwaṭṭaʾ* = Mālik b. Anas. *Al-Muwaṭṭaʾ*. Ed. Muḥammad Fuʾād ʿAbd al-Bāqī. Beirut, 1985.

Mufīd, *Irshād* = Al-Shaykh al-Mufīd, Muḥammad b. Muḥammad b. al-Nuʿmān al-ʿUkbarī. *Al-Irshād fī maʿrifat ḥujaj Allāh ʿalā al-ʿibād*. Beirut, 1993.

—— *Tafḍīl* = Al-Shaykh al-Mufīd, Muḥammad b. Muḥammad b. al-Nuʿmān al-ʿUkbarī. *Tafḍīl Amīr al-Muʾminīn*. Ed. ʿAlī Mūsā al-Kaʿbī. Beirut, 1993.

Al-Qāḍī al-Nuʿmān, *Daʿāʾim* = Al-Qāḍī al-Nuʿmān b. Muḥammad. *Daʿāʾim al-Islām*. Ed. Asaf A. A. Fyzee. Cairo, 1951–1969.

—— *Majālis* = Al-Qāḍī al-Nuʿmān b. Muḥammad. *Al-Majālis wa-l-musāyarāt*. Ed. al-Faqī, Shabbūḥ and Yaʿlāwī. Beirut, 1997.

—— *Uṣūl* = Al-Qāḍī al-Nuʿmān b. Muḥammad. *Kitāb ikhtilāf uṣūl al-madhāhib*. Ed. S. T. Lokhandwalla. Simla, 1972.

Shahrastānī, *Milal* = Al-Shahrastānī, Muḥammad b. ʿAbd al-Karīm. *Al-Milal wa-l-niḥal*. Ed. Muḥammad Sayyid Kaylānī. Beirut, 1404 (AH).

Ṭabarānī, *Awsaṭ* = Al-Ṭabarānī, Sulaymān b. Aḥmad. *Al-Muʿjam al-awsaṭ*. Ed. Ṭāriq b. ʿAwaḍ Allāh and ʿAbd al-Ḥasan b. Ibrāhīm. Beirut, 1995.

Zamakhsharī, *Fāʾiq* = Al-Zamakhsharī, Jār Allāh Maḥmūd b. ʿUmar. *Al-Fāʾiq fī gharīb al-ḥadīth*. Ed. Muḥammad Abū al-Faḍl Ibrāhīm and ʿAlī Muḥammad al-Bījāwī. Cairo, 1979.

Secondary Sources

Brunschvig, "Argumentation" = Brunschvig, Robert. "Argumentation Fāṭimīde contre le raisonnement juridique par analogie, *Qiyās*". *Recherches Islamologiques, recueil d'articles offert à Georges Anawati et Louis Gardet par leurs collègues et amis*. Louvain 1997, pp. 75–84.

Cortese, *Collection* = Cortese, Delia. *Arabic Ismaili Manuscripts. The Zāhid ʿAlī Collection in the library of the Institute of Ismaili Studies*. London, 2003.
Daftary, *History and Thought* = Daftary, Farhad ed. *Medieval Ismaʿili History and Thought*. Cambridge, 2001.
Dachraoui, "Muʿizz" = Dachraoui, Farhat. "Al-Muʿizz li-Dīn Allāh". *EI*².
——, "Al-Nuʿmān" = Dachraoui, Farhat. "Al-Nuʿmān b. Abī ʿAbd Allh b. Manṣūr b. Ḥayyūn". *EI*².
*EI*² = *Encyclopedia of Islam*. Second Edition. CD ROM Edition. Leiden.
Goriawala, *Catalogue* = Goriawala, Muʿizz. *A Descriptive Catalogue of the Fyzee Collection of Ismaili Manuscripts*. Bombay: University of Bombay, 1965.
Halm, *Empire* = Halm, Heinz. *The Empire of the Mahdi: The Rise of the Fatimids*. Translated from the German by Michael Bonner. Leiden, 1996.
——, *Learning* = Halm, Heinz. *The Fatimids and their Traditions of Learning*. London, 2001.
Hamdani, *Revolution* = Sumaiya A. Hamdani. *Between Revolution and State: The Path to Fatimid Statehood*. London 2006.
Kazimirski = Kazimirski, A. de B. *Dictionnaire Arabe Français*. Paris, 1860. Réimpression, Beirut, n.d.
Lecomte, *Divergences* = Lecomte, Gérard. *Le Traité des Divergences du ḥadīṯ d'Ibn Qutayba*. Damascus, 1962.
——, "Introduction" = Lecomte, Gérard. "L'introduction du *Kitāb Adab al-Kātib* d'Ibn Qutayba". *Mélanges Massignon*, tome III. Damascus, 1957, pp. 45–64.
——, *Ibn Qutayba* = Lecomte, Gérard. *Ibn Qutayba. L'Homme, Son Œuvre, Ses Idées*. Damascus, 1965.
Madelung and Walker, *Advent* = Madelung Wilferd and Paul Walker. *The Advent of the Fatimids*. London, 2000.
Poonawala, *Biobibliography* = Poonawala, Ismail K. *Biobibliography of Ismāʿīli Literature*. Malibu, California, 1977.
——, "Jurisprudence" = Poonawala, Ismail K. "Al-Qāḍī al-Nuʿmān and Ismaʿili Jurisprudence", in *Medieval Ismaʿili History and Thought* (ed. F. Daftary) Cambridge, 2001, pp. 117–143.
Sellheim, "al-Ḳālī" = Sellheim, Rudolph. "Al-Ḳālī, Abū ʿAlī Ismāʿīl b. al-Ḳāsim". *EI*².
Soravia, "Préface" = Soravia, Bruna. "Ibn Qutayba en al-Andalus. La Préface à l'*Adab al-Kātib* dans le Commentaire d'Ibn al-Sīd al-Baṭalyawsī". *Al-Qanṭara*, vol. XXV, Madrid, 2004, pp. 539–565.

www.ingramcontent.com/pod-product-compliance
Lightning Source LLC
LaVergne TN
LVHW011130300926
849160LV00008B/585
* 9 7 8 9 0 0 4 2 0 9 8 1 7 *

رسالة ذات البيان
في الردّ على ابن قتيبة

تأليف

القاضي النعمان بن محمد

(ت ٣٦٣/٩٧٤)

حققها وعلق عليها وقدم لها

أبراهام حكيم

TUTA SUB AEGIDE PALLAS · 1683 ·

بريل

الناشر

دار بريل للنشر في ليدن المحروسة وبوسطن

سنة ٢٠١٢

محتويات

رسالة ذات البيان في الردّ على ابن قتيبة

الجزء الثامن:

الجزء التاسع:

[مقدمة المؤلف][1]

| بسم الله الرحمن الرحيم. الحمد لله رب العالمين وصلى الله على سيّدنا ٢أ
محمد وآله الأكرمين[2]

أسعدك الله بطاعته واستعملك بمرضاته ووفّقك الله لما يرضيه[3] ويرضي وليّه وأعانك على ما استكفاك وأقامك له.

كنت أحضرتني، أحضرك[4] الله التوفيق، كتاب عبد الله بن مسلم بن قتيبة الذي ألّفه في تقويم اللسان واليد والإعراب وسمّاه كتاب آداب الكتّاب.[5] وذكرت لي أنّك أخذت الأمراء، السادة ولد أمير المؤمنين، مولانا وسيّدنا صلوات الله عليه، بحفظه لما فيه من فنون العلم والمعرفة، وأثبتّ لهم مجمله وأوضحت لهم مشكله وفتحت لهم مقفله ليفهموه وليعلموا علم ما فيه.

وإنّك وقفت منه على فصل فيه ذكر جمل من القول في الفقه سألتني عن
معانيها لتبيّن لهم ذلك فيما أبنته وتثبّته لهم فيما أثبتّه حسبما صنعت | من ٢ب

---

[1] أضفنا هذا العنوان على الأصل. وفي ف: الجزء الأوّل من رسالة ذات البيان.

[2] هذه العبارة كتبت في هامش الأصل وبخط مغاير.

[3] في المخطوطتين: يرضيك، ونرجّح أنّ ما أثبتناه هو الصحيح.

[4] في المخطوطتين: وأحضرك، ونرجّح أنّ ما أثبتناه هو الصحيح.

[5] في هامش الأصل وبخط مغاير: أدب آداب الكتّاب، أدب آداب الكاتب (نسخة مطبوعة).

ذلك فيما وقفت عليه وعرفته. وقرأت عليّ الفصل من الكتاب وأجبتك عما سألت عنه من بيان ما فيه وشرحتُ لك معانيه وأوقفتك على الصحيح من غير الصحيح منه، فسألتَ بسط ذلك لك في كتاب ليكون أثبت للحفظ وأوضح في البيان وأسلم من الزيادة والنقصان. فرأيتُ بسط ذلك كما سألتَ ليكون أبلغ في معرفة ما يستفيده الأمراء أنماهم الله وبلغ وليّه فيهم وفي كلّ الأمور ما يؤمله بمنّه وفضله وأنجز له ما وعده.

ذكر الفصل الذي سألت بيان ما فيه

أُثبِتُ ما في هذا الفصل أوّلا على حسبما هو في الكتاب المُقَدّم ذكره ليكون البيان على فصوله فصلا فصلا إن شاء الله.

ذكر ابن قتيبة في هذا الكتاب ما ينبغي لطالب العلم والأدب أن يعلمه ويأخذ نفسه بحفظه وتعلمه، فذكر وجوها من العلوم، ثم قال:

٣أ ولا بدّ | له من النظر في جمل الفقه ومعرفة أصوله من حديث رسول الله صلى الله عليه وعلى آله[٦] وصحابته كقوله:

البيّنة على المدّعي واليمين على المدّعى عليه، والخراج[٧] بالضمان، وجُرح العَجْماء جُبار، ولا يغلق الرهن، والمنحة مردودة، والعاريّة مؤدّاة، والزعيم غارم، ولا وصيّة لوارث، ولا قطع في ثمر ولا كثر، ولا قود إلا بحديدة، والمرأة تعاقل الرجل إلى ثلث ديتها، ولا تعقل العاقلة عمدًا ولا عبدًا ولا صلحًا ولا اعترافًا، ولا طلاق في إغلاق، والبيّعان بالخيار ما لم يفترقا، والجار أحقّ بصقبه، والطلاق بالرجال والعِدّة بالنساء، وكَنَهْيِهِ في البيوع عن المخابرة والمحاقلة والمزابنة والمعاومة والثنيا، وعن ربح ما لم يُضْمَن، وعن بيع ما لم يُقْبَض، وعن بَيعتَيْن في بيعة،

[٦] وعلى آله: إضافة في الأصل على عبارة أدب الكاتب وهي غير مثبتة في ف.

[٧] كتب فوقها في الأصل بخط مغاير: الخرج.

٣ب وعن الشَرطَيْن[٨] في بيع، وعن بيع وسَلَف، وعن بيع الغَرَر وعن | بيع المواصفة، وعن الكالئ [بالكالئ]،[٩] وعن تلقّي الركبان.[١٠]

ذكر البيان على[١١] إغفال ابن قتيبة فيما بسطه قبل هذا الفصل مما ذكره أنه ينبغي لطالب العلم أن يعلمه ويأخذ به نفسه.

إعلم، حفظك اللّٰه، أنّ عبد اللّٰه بن مسلم بن قتيبة، وإن كان عند أهل العلم باللسان ثقة فيما وداه من ذلك عن المتقدمين من أهل العلم به وحسن التأليف فيما جمعه وألفه منه، فإنّه ليس بالثقة ولا بالمأمون عند العلماء بالفقه ولا هو من أهله. وهو مع ذلك عدوّ من أعداء اللّٰه وأعداء أوليائه، شديد النصب والطعن على الحقّ وأهله، حشويّ، عاميّ، يذهب إلى التشبيه ويدفع إمامة أهل بيت رسول اللّٰه صلى اللّٰه عليه وعليهم ويثبت إمامة أعدائهم، ويخرج في ذلك عن حدود أكثر العامّة. حتى أنّه ذكر في كتابه الذي سمّاه كتاب

٤أ المعارف الحسين بن علي | صلوات اللّٰه عليهما فقال:

---

[٨] في أدب الكاتب: شرطين.

[٩] أضيفت في هامش الأصل بخط مغاير.

[١٠] ابن قتيبة، أدب الكاتب، ص ١٣–١٤.

[١١] كتبت في هامش الأصل بنفس الخط.

وأما حسين فكان يكنى أبا عبد الله وخرج على يزيد فوجّه إليه عبيد الله بن زياد عمر[١٢] بن سعد بن أبي وقاص فقتله سنان بن أبي أنس[١٣] النخعي.[١٤]

فأقام عدوّ الله ابن قتيبة هذا الحسين صلوات الله عليه مقام الخوارج ويزيد اللعين ابن معاوية اللعين مقام الأئمّة، كما يعتقد ذلك هو وأهل مذهبه. وكما حُكِيَ عن مالك بن أنس أنّه قال: ما كنت أحبّ لعليّ[١٥] الخروج على معاوية. ولولا أن يطول الكتاب ويخرج عمّا قصدته به لذكرت ممّا ذكره عدوّ الله ابن قتيبة في كتبه من الزراية والطعن على الأئمّة صلوات الله عليهم وأوليائهم وعلى ما يذهبون إليه كثيرًا من هذا وما يشبهه. فلا ترى، أو من يرى ما جاء عنه من حلال الله وحرامه ودينه وأحكامه أنّه على شيء من الحقّ ولا أنه ممّن يوثَق به أو يؤخذ | بشيء من ذلك عنه. ٤ب

---

[١٢] في المخطوطتين: عمرو، والمعروف أن عمر بن سعد بن أبي وقاص هو الذي وجّهه عبيد الله بن زياد لقتال الحسين بن علي.

[١٣] الأصل و ف: سنان بن قيس النخعي وهو مجهول. وقد أجمعت المصادر أنّ قاتل الحسين هو سنان بن أبي أنس أو سنان بن أنس النخعي.

[١٤] في كتاب المعارف الذي نعتمده اختلاف لما نقله القاضي النعمان هنا. قال ابن قتيبة في المعارف ص ٢١٣: وأما الحسين بن علي بن أبي طالب فكان يكنى أبا عبد الله. وخرج يريد الكوفة فوجه إليه عبيد الله بن زياد عمر بن سعد بن أبي وقاص فقتله سنان بن أبي أنس النخعي سنه إحدى وستين. راجع تعليقاتنا حول هذا الاختلاف ضمن ملاحظاتنا على مقدمة القاضي في دراستنا التمهيديّة لمقدّمة هذه الرسالة.

[١٥] في الأصل أضيفت العبارة لعلي بعد أحبّ بخط مغاير وهي ضمن النصّ في ف. راجع تعليقاتنا على هذه الإضافة في دراستنا التمهيديّة لمقدّمة هذه الرسالة.

وأما قوله: ولا بدّ من النظر في جمل الفقه ومعرفة أصوله من حديث رسول الله صلى الله عليه وعلى آله[٦] وصحابته، ثم ذكر هذه الجمل التي بسطناها عنه بعد أن قدّم ذكر وجوه من العلوم حضّ عليها وأمر بتعلمها. واقتصر بالتعلم من علم الفقه على ما ذكره في هذا الفصل وزعم أن ذلك يغنيه عن كثير من إطالة الفقهاء، فإنّ ذلك من تخلفه عن علم الفقه ورغبته عنه وزهادته فيه. وكان أولى أن يبتدئ به فيما يحضّ المتعلم عليه، ثم بما يلزمه أن يعلمه منه ممّا تعبدّ الله عزّ وجلّ العباد بعلمه لإقامة ما افترضه عليهم من دينه الذي تعبدّهم به، ولا يقتصر بمن حضّه على طلب العلم بما اقتصر به عليه من هذه الجمل ويزعم أنها تغنيه عن غيرها منه.

٥أ وكان الذي ينبغي أن يحضّه منه عليه، بعد توحيد الله عزّ وجلّ ومعرفة | أوليائه الذين بهم تقبل الأعمال، بما هو متعبّد به من واجب الطهارة والصلاة والزكاة والصوم والحجّ والجهاد. فهذه دعائم الإسلام التي بُنيَ عليها. فإذا علم ذلك علم ما تعبدّه الله عزّ وجلّ بأن يعلمه، نظر أيضًا فيما أحله الله عزّ وجلّ وحرّمه عليه ليأتي من ذلك ما يحلّ ويجتنب ما يحرّم.

[٦] وعلى آله: كذا الأصل وليست في نصّ كتّاب المعارف ولا في ف.

ثم هو بعد ذلك مرغب في طلب العلم. فقد جاء عن رسول الله صلى الله عليه وعلى آله أنّه قال: طلب العلم فريضة على كلّ مسلم ومسلمة.[١٧] وقال: أربع تلزم كل ذي حِجى وعقل من أمتي: استماع العلم وحفظه والعمل به ونشره.[١٨] وقال: اطلبوا العلم ولو بالصين.[١٩]

وعن عليّ صلوات الله عليه أنه قال: إذا عقل الغلام وعرف القرآن عُلِّم الصلاة.[٢٠] وقال: يجب الصلاة على الصبيّ إذا عقل والصوم إذا أطاق،[٢١] يعني عليه السلام وجوب ندب وتعليم لا وجوب فرض وإلزام لأن الفروض لا تجب إلا على | البالغين المكلفين. ٥ب

ولكن يجب أن يُعَلَّم الأطفال الطهارة والصوم والصلاة وما يلزمهم من الفرائض قبل أن يبلغوا ليكونوا قد عرفوا ذلك، فإذا وجب عليهم أتوا منه ما يعرفون.

ورُوي عن أبي جعفر محمد بن عليّ بن الحسين صلوات الله عليه أنّه سئل عن الصبيّ متى يصلي فقال: إذا عقل الصلاة.[٢٢]

---

[١٧] الكليني، الكافي، ج ١ ص ٣٠. القاضي النعمان، دعائم الإسلام، ج ١ ص ٨٤.

[١٨] القاضي النعمان، دعائم الإسلام، ج ١ ص ١٨٠.

[١٩] المجلسي، بحار الأنوار، ج ١ ص ١٧٧.

[٢٠] القاضي النعمان، دعائم الإسلام، ج ١ ص ١٩٣.

[٢١] المرجع السابق، نفس الجزء والصفحة.

[٢٢] الكليني، الكافي، ج ٣ ص ٢٠٦.

وقال رسول الله صلى الله عليه وعلى آله: مروا صبيانكم بالصلاة إذا كانوا أبناء سبع سنين، واضربوهم عليها إن تركوها إذا بلغوا تسعًا، وإذا أطاقوا الصلاة فلا تؤخّروهم عن الصلاة المكتوبة.[٢٣]

وعن جعفر بن محمد صلوات الله عليه أنّه قال: لو أُتيتُ بشابّ من شيعتنا لم يتفقه لأحسنت أدبه،[٢٤] في كثير من الرغائب في الفقه والأمر بتعلمه يخرج ذكرها عن حدّ هذا الكتاب.[٢٥]

فكان ينبغي لابن قتيبة أن يحضّ من حضّه[٢٦] على طلب العلم على أن يطلب
٦أ منه أوّلا [...][٢٧] | ويتعلم ما يقيم فرضه الذي افترضه الله عزّ وجلّ عليه، إذ لا بدّ له من علم ذلك، فيذكر له ما يجب عليه أن يعلمه من فروض طهارته وصلاته وما قد قدّمنا ذكره من ذلك، ولا يقتصر به على علم هذه الجُمَل التي ذكرها ويزعم أن ذلك يغنيه من تطويل الفقهاء بزعمه. وتطويل الفقهاء علم كلّه، ومن زعم أن العلم يُستَغنى عنه فلم يدرِ قدر العلم ولا عرفه.

---

[٢٣] القاضي النعمان، دعائم الإسلام، ج ١ ص ١٩٤.

[٢٤] القاضي النعمان، دعائم الإسلام، ج ١ ص ١٨٠. وأورده الكليني عن الباقر بلفظ مغاير: راجع الكافي، ج ١ ص ٧.

[٢٥] في المخطوطتين: عن حد هذا العلم. ونرجّح أنّ ما أثبتناه هو الصحيح.

[٢٦] الأصل: حظه وهو تحريف.

[٢٧] يبدو أنّ هاهنا نقصا في المخطوطتين.

وأيّ مقام أخزى من مقام من علم هذه الجمل التي ذكرها ابن قتيبة وزعم أنّها تغني عن جملة العلم ثم توضّأ واغتسل أو تيمّم فلم يدرِ كيف يتوضّأ ويغتسل ويتيمّم، أو صلى فلم يدرِ كيف يصلي، أو سئل عن مسألة من أمر دينه فلم يدرِ ما الجواب فيها.

وقد رُوي أنّ رسول الله صلى الله عليه وعلى آله قيل له في بعض غزواته إنّ عمّار بن ياسر عريانا يتمعّك في التراب، فأرسل إليه فأتاه وقال له: يا عمّار ما لك تتمعّك كما يتمعّك | الحمار؟ فقال: يا رسول الله أصابتني ٦ب جنابة فلم أجد الماء، فتبسّم رسول الله صلى الله عليه وعلى آله وقال: يا عمّار يجزيك من ذلك ضربة تضرب باطن كفّيْكَ بها على الأرض فتمسح بها وجهك وضربة أخرى تمسح بها يديك بكلّ واحدة منها على الأخرى.[٢٨] فلو كان عمّار رضي الله عنه قد طلب علم ذلك لوجده في ظاهر كتاب الله جلّ ذكره.

وكذلك أئمّة ابن قتيبة، هذا الجاهل، قد اخطأوا في كثير من الأحكام وغلطوا في كثير من الفتيا في الحلال والحرام وكثير من أصحابه المنتحلين

---

[٢٨] لم أعثر على هذا الحديث بلفظه فيما بين يدي من مصادر. قارن: الطبراني، المعجم الأوسط، ج ٢ ص ١٣.

نحلته وكثير ممن لم يتفقه في الدين واقتصر على علم ما حضّه هو عليه وزعم أنّه يغنيه. كما أمر أبو بكر بقطع ضيف سارق، والضيف لا يُقطع، وأمر عمر برجم حامل زَنتْ، والحامل لا تُرجَم حتى تضع، في كثير يطول ذكره ويخرج عن حدّ هذا الكتاب استقصاؤه من مثل ذلك ما جاء عنهم.

١٧أ وكمثل ما بلغنا وشاهدناه من أهل عصرنا من جلة[٢١] | ابن قتيبة هذا، نحو ما سأل أبو عبد الله صاحب دعوة المغرب بعضَ من كان يتقلد الحكومة في مدينة القيروان من المالكيّين عمّا كان يحكم به، فقال: أحكم بالسنّة. قال له أبو عبد الله: وما السنّة؟ قال: كلام الله وليس بمخلوق. فتضاحك عليه من سمعه من الألبّاء وخجل هو وأصحابه الذين حضروه وصار حديثاً من أجل ذلك.

وكما ذُكر عن آخر منهم وقع في العراقيّين ينتقصهم، فقال له بعضهم ممن عرف جهله وتخلفه: أصلحك الله، كم يجب في مائتي درهم من الزكاة؟ فسكت ساعة ثم قال: درهمين. فقال له الرجل: فمن لم يعلم ما يجب في مائتي درهم من الزكاة ينتقص العلماء ويقع فيهم؟

---

[٢١] لعله سقطت من المخطوطين كلمة "أصحاب" بعد هذه العبارة.

وكما ذكر عن آخر منهم استحكمه بعض القضاة، فسأله يومًا عمّا حكم به في يومه ذلك فقال: حكمت اليوم على غائب، فقال: أصبت السنّة. ثم سأله عن المكان الذي هو به غائب فذكر موضعًا تكون مسافته | قدر ٧ب
ميلين، فقال: إنّا لله! ويحك فضحتنا! ليس من غاب بمثل هذا الموضع يكون ممّن يُحْكَمُ عليه وهو غائب. في كثير من مثل هذا ممّا جاء عن مثل من اقتصر من الفقه على ما أمر ابن قتيبة بالاقتصار عليه وعلى ما هو أضعاف ذلك إذا جهل غيره مما يلزمه علمه.

وكما ذكر عن بعض أهل النسب الشريف أنّه مرّ بقوم قد وضعوا جنازة يريدون الصلاة عليها، فلمّا رأوه أعظموه ودعوه ليقدّموه على الصلاة عليها، فلم يمكنه التخلف ولم يدرِ كيف الصلاة على الجنائز، فتقدّم وكبّر وركع كما يفعل في الصلاة المكتوبة. فوقف القوم ثم كبّر بعد أن رفع رأسه من الركوع وسجد فجبذوا بثوبه من ورائه وأزالوه وقالوا له: ليس هكذا أيّها الشريف يُصلى على الجنائز. فصار حديثًا من أجل ذلك. ثم تقدّم بعضهم فصلى على الجنازة ووقف هو خجلا فصلى بصلاته.[٣٠]

---

[٣٠] لم نعثر على هذه الروايات الأربع فيما بين أيدينا من مصادر.

فأوّل ما ينبغي أن يتعلم من العلم ما لا يسع جهله من الفقه وما يلزم العمل به
٨أ في | الدّين، ثم ما زاد المتعلم من ذلك كان أشرف له وأفضل. قال الله جل
من قائل: ﴿يَرْفَعِ اللَّهُ الَّذِينَ آمَنُوا مِنكُمْ وَالَّذِينَ أُوتُوا الْعِلْمَ دَرَجَاتٍ﴾[٣١] وقال:
﴿هَلْ يَسْتَوِي الَّذِينَ يَعْلَمُونَ وَالَّذِينَ لا يَعْلَمُونَ إِنَّمَا يَتَذَكَّرُ أُوْلُوا الأَلْبَابِ﴾[٣٢].
وقال علي صلوات الله عليه: قيمة كل امرئ ما كان يحسن[٣٣].

---

[٣١] المجادلة ٥٨/١١.
[٣٢] الزمر ٣٩/٩.
[٣٣] المجلسي، بحار الأنوار، ج ٤ ص ١٦٥–١٦٦.

ذكر بيان قوله:
البيّنة على المدّعي واليمين على المدّعى عليه[٣٤]

هذا قول ثابت عن النبي صلى الله عليه وعلى آله في الدعوى في الأموال. وهو أنّ من ادّعى شيئًا منها على آخر، فأنكر المدّعى عليه دعواه والذي يُدّعى عليه به في يديه، أنّ البيّنة على المدّعي. فإن أتى ببيّنة وعدلت، وكان ذلك عند حاكم، عرّف الحاكم[٣٥] المدّعى عليه ما ثبت عنده من شهادة البيّنة عليه وسأله عن منفعة إن كانت في ذلك عنده. فإن جاء بما يبطل تلك الشهادة من تجريح البيّنة أو ما يبطل شهادتهم، أو سقوط[٣٦] ما شهدوا
٨ب به وزواله عنه ببيّنة تشهد ذلك له، | أو بإقرار المدعي بالبراءة للمدّعى
عليه، سقط ذلك عنه. فإن لم يأت بشيء من ذلك بعد أن يستنفذ الحاكم حججه ويعذر إليه في ذلك على قدر ما يرى أنه يطلب منافعه، عرّفه أنه يحكم عليه وأنّ له إن شاء أن يستحلف المدّعي على دعواه مع بيّنة، إن كان

---

[٣٤] قارن بحث القاضي النعمان لهذه المسألة باختصار: دعائم الإسلام، ج ٢ ص ٤٢٨.

[٣٥] في الأصل: أضيفت كلمة الحاكم فوق عَرّفَ بخط مغاير.

[٣٦] أضيفت في هامش الأصل.

[ذلك][٣٧] فيما جرى بينهما بدعوى المدّعي. فإن طلب يمينه عرض الحاكم اليمين على المدّعي أنّ له ما شهدت له البيّنة به. فإن حلف حكم له وإن امتنع من اليمين لم يحكم له بشيء، إلا أن يكون تلك الدعوى من شيء يدور على المدّعى عليه لا يعلم المدّعي حقيقته، مثل أن يكون ذلك من ميراث دار إليه، أو إقرار أقرّ له المدعى عليه[٣٨] به، أو من جناية، أو سرقة، أو ما أشبه ذلك، فإنّ ذلك ليس عليه فيه يمين، إلا أن يشاء المدعى عليه أن يستحلفه
١٩أ أنّه لا يعلم أنّ شيئًا سقط عنه من هذا الذي | شهد له به [عليه]،[٣٩] ولا أنّ الشهادة فيه باطل في علمه، فعليه أن يحلف بذلك. فإن لم يحلف لم يقض له بشيء. وهذا قول أهل البيت صلوات الله عليهم ووافقهم عليه كثير من فقهاء العامّة. فقد صارت اليمين هاهنا على المدّعي في ظاهر الأمر إلا أنها في باطنه في الدعوى عليه بسقوط ما وجب له.

وقوله البيّنة على المدّعي أيضًا قول مجمل يعني به أنّ ذلك عليه إن طلب الدعوى وليس ذلك عليه بواجب أن يأتي بالبيّنة طُلِبَ أو لم يُطلَب وأن يؤخذ

---

[٣٧] ناقصة في الأصل وأثبتناها من ف.

[٣٨] الأصل: أضيفت كلمة عليه فوق كلمة المدّعي بخط مغاير وهي مثبتة في ف.

[٣٩] ناقصة في الأصل وأثبتناها من ف.

بذلك كما يؤخذ بما عليه من الواجب. وهذا اجتماع[٤٠] لا اختلاف فيه بين المسلمين.

وقد يكتب بعض الجهّال من القضاة والحُكام في محاضرهم وأحكامهم إذا ذكر المدّعي ودعواه[٤١] فيقول: فأمرته أن يحضر البيّنة على ما ادّعاه. وهذا القول خطأ لأنّ أمر الحاكم حُكم ولا يجب أن يأمر إلا بما يجب ويلزم.

وكذلك يقولون في مجالسهم للمدّعي: أحضر البيّنة، | إذا أنكر المدّعى ٩ب
عليه، وذلك خطأ. وإنما ينبغي أن يقال له: ألك البيّنة على دعواك؟ فإن قال نعم قيل له: فأحضرها إن شئت، أو يقول: أنا أحضر البيّنة، فيؤذن له في ذلك، ويُكتَب في المحضر والحكم: فسألته عن بيّنة إن كانت له ولا يُقال: أمرته.

وهذا الذي ذكرته كلّه قول أهل البيت صلوات الله عليهم وقول كثير ممن وافقهم من فقهاء العامة.

وخالفهم بعضهم في يمين المدعي مع بيّنته وقالوا: ليس على المدّعي يمين إذا أقام البيّنة لأنّ رسول الله صلى الله عليه وعلى آله لم يوجب ذلك عليه، وإنما أوجب اليمين على المدّعى عليه. واحتجّ من ذهب إلى ذلك بأنّ الدعوى

---

[٤٠] كذا في المخطوطتين ولعل الصواب: إجماع.

[٤١] أضيفت في الأصل فوق كلمة المدّعي بخط مغاير.

قد تسقط عن المدّعى عليه من حيث يعلم ومن حيث لا يعلم، فمن حقّه أن يستحلف الذي ادّعى عليه أنّ الذي ادّعاه له بحقّ ثابت عليه ما سقط عنه [منه][٤٢] قليل ولا كثير.

١٠أ وحجّتنا نحن عليهم وعلى جميع من خالف ما جاء عن أئمّتنا صلوات الله | عليهم أجمعين أنّ الذي جاء عنهم إنّما نقلوه عن رسول الله صلى الله عليه وعلى آله وأخذ عنه واحد بعد واحد منهم، ليس كما تقول به العامّة من رأيها[٤٣] وقياسها واستحسانها في دين الله عزّ وجلّ وأحكامه ما تقول به.

وليس فيما جاء عن رسول الله صلى الله عليه ولا فيما جاء عن أئمّة دينه لقائل اعتراض لأنّ الله جلّ من قائل يقول: ﴿وَمَا آتَاكُمُ الرَّسُولُ فَخُذُوهُ وَمَا نَهَاكُمْ عَنْهُ فَانتَهُوا﴾،[٤٤] وقال: ﴿أَطِيعُواْ اللَّهَ وَأَطِيعُواْ الرَّسُولَ وَأُوْلِي الأَمْرِ مِنكُمْ﴾.[٤٥] وإنما يلزم الاعتراض من قال في دين الله برأيه[٤٦] وقياسه واستحسانه كما قالت العامّة بذلك.

[٤٢] ناقصة في الأصل وأثبتناها من ف.

[٤٣] في المخطوطتين: راءها.

[٤٤] الحشر ٧/٥٩.

[٤٥] النساء ٤/٥٩.

[٤٦] في المخطوطتين: برائها.

وفي قوله البيّنة على المدّعي واليمين على المدّعى عليه وجه آخر: وهو أنّ ذلك ليس في كل شيء، وإنما قاله رسول الله صلّى الله عليه وعلى آله في شيء دون شيء، لأنّ من ادّعى على رجل أنه قذفه أو أتى | إليه أو ١٠ب إلى غيره ما يوجب عليه حدًّا أو تعزيرًا أو أدبًا، ولم تكن له بيّنة، وسأل استحلاف من ادّعى ذلك عليه، لم يلزم[٤٧] في ذلك على المدّعى عليه يمين لأنّه إن نكل عن اليمين لم يلزمه الحدّ بالنكول.

وقد روى الأئمّة من أهل بيت رسول الله صلى الله عليه وعلى آله عنه أنّه نهى أن يُحْلَفَ في الحدود. وقال عليّ صلوات الله عليه: لا يُسْتَحْلفُ في الحدود.[٤٨] وأنّ رجلا أتاه برجل فقال: هذا افترى عليّ. فسأل المّدعى عليه فأنكر الدعوى. فقال للمدّعي: ألك بيّنة؟ قال لا. قال: فَخَلِّه. قال: فاستَحْلِفْهُ لي يا أمير المؤمنين. فقال: لا يمين في حدّ ولا قصاص في عظم.[٤٩] يعني أنّ من كسر عظمًا لم يُقتصّ منه بكسر عظم مثله لأنّ ذلك لا يوصل إليه بحقيقته ولكنّه يلزم الدية الواجبة في ذلك.

---

[٤٧] في المخطوطتين: تلزم.

[٤٨] لم نعثر على هذه العبارة بلفظها منسوبة إلى الإمام عليّ فيما بين أيدينا من مصادر.

[٤٩] الكليني، الكافي ج ٧ ص ٢٥٦؛ القاضي النعمان، دعائم الإسلام، ج ٢، ص ٤٦٦.

كذلك لا يُقضى في الحدود بشهادة على شهادة ولا بكتاب قاض إلى قاض.[٥٠]

١١أ رُويَ ذلك عن أبي عبد الله | جعفر بن محمد صلوات الله عليه وعلى آبائه أنّه قال: لا يمين في حدّ.[٥١] ووافق ذلك جماعة من أهل الفتيا من العامّة وقالوا به. وخالفه آخرون وقالوا: يجب الأيمان في الحدود.

وقد ذكرنا أنّ ذلك جاء عن رسول الله صلى الله عليه وعن الأئمّة من ذرّيّته وأنّه لا يجب الاعتراض على ما ثبت عنهم. وإنّما خالفهم في ذلك من أثبت الخبر الأوّل عن رسول الله ولم يعلم ما استثناه في الحدود، وعلى من لم يعلم ذلك ولم يبلغه[٥٢] أن يأخذه عمّن بلغه ذلك وعلمه.

وفي ذلك أيضًا وجه آخر وهو أنّ البيّنة في الدماء على المدّعى عليه واليمين على المدّعي إذا جاء بلطخ. ومن ذلك حكم القسامة أنّ رسول الله صلى الله عليه وعلى آله قضى بها. وذلك أنّ رجلا من الأنصار قُتِلَ في بعض حوائط خيبر فأتى أولياؤه إلى رسول الله صلى الله عليه وعلى آله وقالوا: يا
١١ب رسول الله اليهود أهل خيبر قتلوا أخانا فأصيب قتيلا في | بعض حوائطهم. فسأل اليهود عن دعواهم فأنكروها. فقال رسول الله صلى الله عليه وعلى آله للأنصار: ألكم بيّنة على دعواكم؟ قالوا: ومن يشهد لنا بذلك وإنّما قتلوه

---

[٥٠] الطوسي، المبسوط، ج ٥ ص ٢٨٨.
[٥١] لم نعثر على هذا الحديث بلفظه رواية عن الإمام جعفر الصادق فيما بين أيدينا من مصادر.
[٥٢] أضيفت في هامش الأصل بنفس الخط.

خفية؟ قال: فتُقسمون خمسين يمينًا على من قتله أقيدكم[٥٣] منه برُمَّته. قالوا: وكيف نقسم على ما[٥٤] لم نره ولم نشهده؟ قال: فيحلف لكم من تدّعون عليه. قالوا: يا رسول الله هم يهود لا يبالون ما حلفوا عليه. قال: فليس لكم غير هذا. ووداه رسول الله من بيت مال المسلمين لئلا يُطَلَّ دم امرئ مسلم.[٥٥] وقال عليّ صلوات الله عليه: قضى رسول الله صلى الله عليه وعلى آله بالقسامة ويمين المدّعي مع الشاهد الواحد في الأموال[٥٦] خاصّة، سُنّة نزل بها جبريل على رسول الله صلى الله عليه وعلى آله.[٥٧] قال جعفر بن محمد صلوات الله عليه: وقضى بها عليّ عليه السلام بالكوفة، ولا يرضى بذلك

---

[٥٣] الأصل: أقدكم وأثبتنا النصّ من ف وهو أصحّ. وقد أخطأ المحقق فيضي فحرّف هذه الكلمة في نصّ دعائم الإسلام وأثبت مكانها كلمة: أقدمكم، مع أنّ الكلمتين أقدكم وأقيدكم ثابتتان في المخطوطات التي اعتمدها في تحقيقه. راجع: القاضي النعمان، دعائم الإسلام، ج ٢ ص ٤٢٨ والحاشية رقم ٣ في نفس الصفحة.

[٥٤] في المخطوطتين: على من لم نره، ونرجّح أنّ ما أثبتناه هو الصواب. وقد أورد القاضي النعمان سؤال الأنصار هذا في الصفحة أدناه برواية: كيف نقسم على ما لم نره.

[٥٥] يروي القاضي هذه الحادثة هنا بإيجاز. وقد أوردها أيضا كذلك في الدعائم ج ٢ ص ٤٢٧–٤٢٨، ثم أوردها مفصلة في ص ٤٢٨–٤٢٩ من الجزء نفسه. راجع الكليني، الكافي، ج ٧ ص ٢٦٢. راجع عنها بتفاصيلها :عبد الرزّاق، المصنف، ج ١٠ ص ٣١–٣٢؛ أحمد، مسند، ج ٤ ص ٣.

[٥٦] أضيفت في هامش الأصل بنفس الخط.

[٥٧] لم نعثر على قول الإمام عليّ هذا بلفظه فيما بين أيدينا من مصادر. قارن: القاضي النعمان، دعائم الإسلام، ج ٢ ص ٤٢٧.

١٢أ لنا عدوّ ولا ينكره لنا وليّ وإنّما القسامة نجاة للناس ولولا ذلك | لقتل الناس بعضهم بعضا إذا خلوا بينهم.[٥٨]

وقال عليه السلام:[٥٩] سألني ابن شبرمة[٦٠] عن القسامة فأخبرته بما قضى به فيها رسول الله صلى الله عليه وعلى آله. قال: فما تقول فيها لو لم يقض فيها رسول الله صلى الله عليه وعلى آله [بشيء]؟[٦١] قال: قلت له: قد أخبرتك بقضاء رسول الله صلى الله عليه وعلى آله فيها وبذلك نقول ونقضي، ولو لم يقض فيها رسول الله صلى الله عليه وعلى آله بشيء لما كان لنا ولا لأحد أن يقضي فيها بشيء من قِبَل رأيه ولا في غيرها.[٦٢]

وإنّما تكون القسامة مع لطخ بشهود وإن لم يبلغوا العدالة وكانوا غير بالغين، أو بتهمة بيّنة وأسباب تدلّ على التهمة كما كانت العداوة بين الأنصار ويهود خيبر ولأنّ الأنصاريّ وُجِدَ قتيلا في حوائطهم ودارهم محضة بهم ليس معهم فيها غيرهم. أو أنّ يقول المقتول قبل أن يموت: فلان قتلني إنْ متّ.[٦٣] فأمّا

١٢ب إذا لم يكن ذلك لم تكن البيّنة إلا على | المدّعي واليمين على المدّعى عليه.

---

[٥٨] : القاضي النعمان، دعائم الإسلام، ج ٢ ص ٤٢٨.

[٥٩] يعني الإمام جعفر الصادق.

[٦٠] هو قاضي الكوفة عبد الله بن شبرمة المتوفى ١٤٤ هـ. راجع عنه: الذهبي، سير، ج ٦ ص ٣٤٧.

[٦١] ناقصة في الأصل واستدركناها من ف.

[٦٢] الكليني، الكافي، ج ٧ ص ٢٦٢.

[٦٣] القاضي النعمان، دعائم الإسلام، ج ٢ ص ٤٢٩.

وإن كان لطخ مما ذكرنا وكان للمتهم بيّنة على[٦٤] براءته قبِلتْ بيّنته[٦٥] ولم تجز القسامة عليه. وذلك مثل أن يشهد له الشهود أنّه كان في وقت القتل معهم أو بمكان لا يمكن أن يصل إلى القتيل في وقت قتله وما أشبه ذلك.

ولا تقسم القسامة إلا ما علمته لأنّ الأنصار لمّا قالوا لرسول الله صلى الله عليه وعلى آله: وكيف نقسم على ما لم نره، لم يقل لهم: لكم ذلك، بل تركهم على ما قالوه منه إذ كان ذلك هو الواجب عنده، ولو كان غيره ممّا هو خلافه يجب لقال لهم ذلك إذ هو مأمور بالبيان، وإنّما يقسم الأولياء الذين يستحقّون الدم. وإن كان من أهل بيت المقتول وقبيلته من لا يستحقّ دمه ولا شيء له فيه ولا يُتهم بحميّة وكان عدلا وشهد على القاتل جازت شهادته.

وأولياء الدم يبدءون بالأَيمان مع اللطخ، فإن لم يحلفوا ولم تقم لهم بيّنة كان على المدّعى عليه أن يحلف إن | سألوا يمينه. فإن لم يحلف كانت الدية ١٣أ
عليه ولم يُقتل بالنكول عن اليمين.

وهذا كلّه قول أهل البيت صلوات الله عليهم ووافقهم على ذلك جماعة من فقهاء العامّة.

---

[٦٤] أضيفت في هامش الأصل.

[٦٥] الأصل: بيّنة، وأثبتنا النصّ من ف وهو أصحّ.

ودفع ذلك آخرون وقالوا: اليمين في كل شيء على المدّعى عليه، إذ جهلوا في ذلك سُنّة رسول الله صلى الله عليه وعلى آله. وقد ذكرنا في المسألة التي قبل هذه المسألة ما يلزم من جهل ذلك ولم يبلغه من الاقتداء بمن علمه وعرفه والرجوع إلى قوله.

وفي ذلك وجه آخر وهو أنّ الله عزّ وجلّ فرض في الدعوى والبيّنات شهادة شاهدَين من الرجال عدلين،[٦٦] ﴿فَإِن لَّمْ يَكُونَا رَجُلَيْنِ فَرَجُلٌ وَامْرَأَتَانِ مِمَّن تَرْضَوْنَ مِنَ الشُّهَدَاء﴾[٦٧] وقال: ﴿وَأَشْهِدُوا ذَوَيْ عَدْلٍ مِّنكُمْ﴾.[٦٨]

وجاء عن الأئمّة من أهل [بيت][٦٩] رسول الله صلوات الله عليهم أنّ رسول الله صلى الله عليه وعلى آله قضى في الأموال خاصة دون غيرها بالشاهد الواحد مع يمين الطالب، وقضى | به عليّ صلوات الله عليه، وقال به الأئمّة ١٣ب
من ولده عليهم السلام.[٧٠] ووافقهم بذلك فريق من فقهاء العامّة. وفارقهم آخرون وقالوا: لا يجوز في الأموال وغيرها إلا شهادة رجلين أو رجل وامرأتين كما

---

[٦٦] في الأصل: أضيفت من الرجال فوق عدلين بخط مغاير.

[٦٧] البقرة ٢/٢٨٢.

[٦٨] الطلاق ٦٥/٢.

[٦٩] ناقصة في الأصل واستدركناها من ف.

[٧٠] راجع: الطوسي، الخلاف، ج ٦ ص ٢٢٧ حيث يورد رواية الإمام جعفر لهذا الحديث عن آبائه عن النبيّ.

قال الله عزّ وجلّ في كتابه، وقد جهلوا ما جاء عن رسول الله صلى الله عليه وعلى آله من ذلك وما رواه الثقات من أهل بيته وغيرهم [من العوامّ].[٧١]

وقد ذكرنا ما يلزم مَن جهل مثل هذا ولم يبلغه من الرجوع إلى قول مَن علمه ورواه من الثقات. وإنّما لزم ذلك لأنّ الله عزّ وجلّ قد ينزل في كتابه ما هو مجمل فيبيّنه الرسول كما افترض الله عزّ وجلّ بيان ذلك عليه بقوله: ﴿وَأَنزَلْنَا إِلَيْكَ الذِّكْرَ لِتُبَيِّنَ لِلنَّاسِ مَا نُزِّلَ إِلَيْهِمْ﴾.[٧٢] والبيان من الرسول عن الله عزّ وجلّ لقوله جلّ من قائل: ﴿وَالنَّجْمِ إِذَا هَوَى. ما ضَلَّ صَاحِبُكُمْ وَمَا غَوَى . وَمَا يَنطِقُ عَنِ الْهَوَى . إِنْ هُوَ إِلاَّ وَحْيٌ يُوحَى . عَلَّمَهُ شَدِيدُ الْقُوَى﴾.[٧٣]

وكذلك قد يأتي عن الرسول صلى الله عليه وعلى آله من القول ما هو مجمل محتاج إلى البيان ممّا ذكره في شيء بعينه فيبيّنه الأئمّة من أهل بيته بما صار إليهم عنه صلى الله عليه وعلى آله من العلم المنقول فيهم عنه. وذلك مثل قوله في هذا الفصل الذي ذكرناه: البيّنة على المدّعي واليمين على المدّعى عليه، إنّما قال ذلك في الدعوى في الأموال على ما بيّنه الأئمّة صلوات الله عليهم إذ هم المبيّنون عنه عن الله عزّ وجلّ مراده فيما أنزله، وأتى على

[٧١] ناقصة في الأصل واستدركناها من ف.

[٧٢] النحل ١٦/٤٤.

[٧٣] النجم ٥٣/١–٥.

لسان رسوله صلى الله عليه وعلى آله، وقد فرض أخذه عنه، فقال تعالى: ﴿وَمَا آتَاكُمُ الرَّسُولُ فَخُذُوهُ وَمَا نَهَاكُمْ عَنْهُ فَانتَهُوا﴾.[٧٤] فكلّ الذي يأتي عن الرسول صلى الله عليه وعلى آله حكمه في القبول كحكم التنزيل، لأنّ التنزيل أوجبه. وكذلك قال جلّ من قائل: ﴿أَطِيعُواْ اللَّهَ وَأَطِيعُواْ الرَّسُولَ
١٤ب وَأُوْلِي الأَمْرِ مِنكُمْ﴾،[٧٥] يعني الأئمّة من أهل بيت | رسول الله صلوات الله عليه وعليهم.

وقد ذكرت ما يوجب ذلك لهم في كتاب أصول المذاهب[٧٦] وغيره بما يخرج عن هذا الكتاب ذكره، فكان ذلك أيضًا ما جاء عنهم صلوات الله عليهم حكمه حكم التنزيل لأنّ التنزيل أوجب طاعتهم وذلك في كل ما أمروا به ونهوا عنه وكانت طاعتهم بذلك موصلة بطاعة الله عزّ وجلّ وطاعة رسوله صلى الله عليه وعلى آله، لا يصلح بعضها إلا ببعض ولا تنفع[٧٧] إلا بأن تنتظم[٧٨] كلّها.

وقد أجمع المسلمون أنّ من أقرّ بالله عزّ وجلّ وزعم أنّه أطاعه وقبل ما جاء عنه، كما زعم من قدّمنا ذكرهم أنهم قبلوا ما جاء في ظاهر القرآن، وأنكر

---

[٧٤] الحشر ٥٩/٧.

[٧٥] النساء ٤/٥٩.

[٧٦] وهو الكتاب المطبوع المعروف باسم "إختلاف أصول المذاهب"

[٧٧] في الأصل: يتقطع، وأضيفت عبارة تنفع في الهامش بنفس الخط.

[٧٨] في المخطوطتين: ينتظم.

الرسول أو ردّ ما جاء عنه كما ردّ هؤلاء ما جاء عنه صلى الله عليه وعلى آله ممّا ذكرناه، وإنْ زعم أنه أقرّ به، لم ينفعه الإقرار بالله وطاعته إذا أنكر الرسول أو دفع ما ثبت عنه أو شيئًا منه. وهم مُلزمون ذلك | غيرَهم وقد ١٥أ
فعلوه. وكذلك يلزمهم مثل ذلك من إنكار أولي الأمر وترك طاعتهم ومخالفتهم ما جاء عنهم واستبدالهم غيرهم بهم. ولا ينفعهم إقرارهم بالله وبرسوله ولا أخذهم عن الرسول إذا عصوا أولي الأمر وخالفوهم لأنّ الله سبحانه جعلها طاعة موصولة فمن قطعها فقد قطع ما أمر الله به أن يوصل. وقد تواعد الله عزّ وجلّ من فعل ذلك بعذابه في كتابه ووعد بثوابه فيه من وصل ما أمر به أن يوصل.

وفي قوله: البيّنة على المدّعي واليمين على المدّعى عليه أيضًا ما هو مجمل في هذا القول، وهو أنّ المراد بذلك العدول من البيّنة والحلف باسم الله عزّ وجلّ ذكره، لا البيّنة غير العدول ولا اليمين بغير الله سبحانه. وهذا ممّا جاء عن الأئمّة من أهل بيت [رسول][79] الله صلوات الله عليه وعلى آله أجمعين ووافقهم عليه جميع المسلمين وجاء في ظاهر الكتاب المبين وقول رسول
| رب العالمين. فمن ذلك قول الله جل من قائل: ﴿وأقسموا بالله جَهْدَ ١٥ب

[79] ناقصة في الأصل واستدركناها من ف.

أَيمانهم﴾[٨٠] وقوله: ﴿وأشهدوا ذَوَيْ عدل منكم﴾،[٨١] وقول رسول الله صلى الله عليه وعلى آله: من كان حالفًا فليحلف بالله أو ليصمت[٨٢] ومن حلف بالله فليَصْدُقْ[٨٣] ومن حُلِفَ له بالله فليقبل فمن لم يفعل فليس بمسلم.[٨٤]

وأجمع أهل الفتيا أنّه لا يُسْتَحْلَفُ من وجبت عليه يمين إلا بالله الذي لا إله إلا هو بما رووه في ذلك عن رسول الله صلى الله عليه وعلى آله ممّا ذكرته، وأنّ اليمين بالمصحف وبالطلاق والعتاق والصدقة والمشي إلى بيت الله الحرام وبغير ذلك من سائر ما يحلف الناس به لا يجب أن يُسْتَحْلَفَ به أحد. وإن سأل ذلك من يجب له اليمين وإن حلف به من حيث وجبت عليه، لم يجز ذلك عنه حتى يحلف بالله عزّ وجلّ.

ثمّ خالف أكثر العامّة ذلك فأوجبوا على من حلف بما نهوا عنه الحنث فيما حلف به عليه إن خالفه أو كذب فيه.

---

[٨٠] الأنعام ٦/١٠٩.

[٨١] الطلاق ٦٥/٢.

[٨٢] الطوسي، الخلاف، ج ٤ ص ٥١٣.

[٨٣] الطوسي، تهذيب الأحكام، ج ٦ ص ٣٤٩.

[٨٤] القاضي النعمان، دعائم الإسلام، ج ٢ ص ٥٢١.

وأبطل ذلك والحنثَ فيه الأئمّة من أهل بيت رسول الله | صلى الله عليه ١٦أ
وعلى آله ورووا ذلك عن رسول الله صلى الله عليه وعلى آله وأوجبوا أنّ الحلف بذلك معصية ومكروه.

وكذلك قال في ذلك المخالفون إلا أنهم أوجبوا به الحنث، وفي ذلك ما يشهد على فساد قولهم. وقد أجمعوا أنّ من حلف على معصية أن يأتيها أو على طاعة أن لا يأتيها أنّ عليه أن يأتي الطاعة ويجتنب المعصية ولا حنث عليه، وهذا ينقض قولهم.

وقد رووا أنّ رسول الله صلى الله عليه وعلى آله خلا بمارية القبطيّة أمته قبل أن يتخذها أم ولد. فاطّلعت عليه عائشة فساءها[٨٥] ذلك وأنكرته، فأراد رسول الله صلى الله عليه وعلى آله أن يرضيها فحرّم مارية على نفسه وحلف لها أنّه لا يأتيها بعد ذلك وأسرّ ذلك إليها. فأطلعت عليه حفصة وتظاهرتا عليه، فأنزل الله عزّ وجلّ في ذلك: ﴿يَا أَيُّهَا النَّبِيُّ لِمَ تُحَرِّمُ مَا أَحَلَّ اللَّهُ لَكَ﴾ إلى قوله: ﴿وَأَبْكَارًا﴾.[٨٦] فكفر رسول الله صلى الله عليه وعلى آله
عن يمينه وأتى مارية وولد منها.[٨٧] | ولو لم يحلف لم يكن عليه كفارة وإنّما ١٦ب

---

[٨٥] أضيفت في هامش الأصل بنفس الخط.

[٨٦] التحريم ٦٦/١–٥.

[٨٧] المعروف في هذه الحادثة غير ما يرويه القاضي النعمان. فقد أورد الطبري في تفسيره أنّ التي أفشت سرّ النبي حفصة بنت عمر وليس عائشة. فروي عن عمر بن الخطاب: وكان بدء الحديث في شأن أم

يلزم الكفارة من حلف على ما له أن يفعله وله أن لا يفعله ففعله، فعليه أن يكفر عن يمينه مثل ما كان لرسول الله صلى الله عليه وعلى آله أن يطأ مارية وله أن لا يطأها إذا لم ير ذلك.

فأمّا من حلف أن لا يصلي أو حلف ليقتلنّ من لا يجب [له][٨٨] قتله أو ما أشبه ذلك فعليه أن يصلي وأن لا يقتل ولا كفارة عليه ولا نذر في ذلك أيضًا.

قال رسول الله صلى الله عليه وعلى آله: لا نذر في معصية.[٨٩]

وفي ذلك أيضًا[٩٠] وجه آخر وهو أنّ الله عزّ وجلّ قال في كتابه: ﴿لاَ يُؤَاخِذُكُمُ اللّهُ بِاللَّغْوِ فِي أَيْمَانِكُمْ وَلَكِن يُؤَاخِذُكُم بِمَا عَقَّدتُّمُ الأَيْمَانَ فَكَفَّارَتُهُ إِطْعَامُ عَشَرَةِ مَسَاكِينَ مِنْ أَوْسَطِ مَا تُطْعِمُونَ أَهْلِيكُمْ أَوْ كِسْوَتُهُمْ أَوْ تَحْرِيرُ رَقَبَةٍ فَمَن لَّمْ يَجِدْ فَصِيَامُ ثَلاَثَةِ أَيَّامٍ ذَلِكَ كَفَّارَةُ أَيْمَانِكُمْ إِذَا حَلَفْتُمْ﴾.[٩١]

إبراهيم القبطية أصابها النبي صلى الله عليه وسلم في بيت حفصة في يومها، فوجدته حفصة فقالت: يا نبي الله لقد جئت إليّ شيئًا ما جئت إلى أحد من أزواجك بمثله في يومي وفي دوري وعلى فراشي. قال: ألا ترضين أن أحرمها فلا أقربها؟ قالت: بلى. فحرمها وقال: لا تذكري ذلك لأحد. فذكرته لعائشة. فأظهره الله عزّ وجلّ عليه، فأنزل الله: ﴿يا أيها النبي لم تحرم ما أحل الله لك تبتغي مرضاة أزوجك﴾ الآيات كلها. فبلغنا أن نبيّ الله صلى الله عليه وسلم كفر يمينه وأصاب جاريته. راجع: الطبري، جامع البيان، ج ٢٨ ص ٢٠١.

[٨٨] ناقصة في الأصل واستدركناها من ف.

[٨٩] الكليني، الكافي، ج ٧ ص ٤٤٠.

[٩٠] أضيفت في هامش الأصل بنفس الخط.

[٩١] المائدة ٥/٨٩.

فلو كانت اليمين بالطلاق والعتاق وغير ذلك ممّا ذكرناه | وأجملنا القول فيه ١٧أ
أَيماناً لكانت هذه كفارتها [كما][٩٢] قال الله عزّ وجلّ، وليس يقول بذلك من
أوجبها أَيمانا فذلك ممّا يفسد ما ذهبوا إليه فيها.

وقول رسول الله صلى الله عليه وعلى آله: واليمين على المدّعى عليه، لا
يقع على ذلك ولا تجزي منه الكفارة من حلف عليه. ويستغفر الله عزّ وجلّ
ويتوب إليه من حلف باسمه كاذبًا وليس عليه في ذلك كفارة.

وكذلك جاء القول عن الأئمّة من أهل بيت رسول الله صلوات الله عليه
وعليهم ووافقهم عليه المنسوبون إلى الفقه بزعمهم من العامّة.

فهذه أصول لما ذكرناه في هذا الفصل ولو فرّعناها لطال القول بتفريعها. وبمثل
هذه الأصول في هذا الباب وفي غيره هي التي يكتفي بها من أراد علم الفقه
وتغنيه عن تطويل الفقهاء، لا ما زعم ابن قتيبة هذا الجاهل أنّ الذي ذكره
يغنيه عن ذلك. وهذه لفظة | واحدة ممّا ذكره من جزء يقلّ إذا تجزّأ ممّا لم ١٧ب
يذكره ممّا يجب أن يعلمه من أراد أن يتفقه في دين الله عزّ وجلّ قد اقتضت
ما ذكرناه [من البيان].[٩٣] ولو لم يكن تَبَيّن ذلك لجرى القول بأنّ اليمين على
المدّعى عليه في جميع ما ذكرنا أنه لا يجزي [فيه][٩٤] وأوجب ذلك من لم

[٩٢] ناقصة في الأصل واستدركناها من ف.

[٩٣] ناقصة في الأصل واستدركناها من ف.

[٩٤] ناقصة في الأصل واستدركناها من ف.

يعلم البيان وقال به، فافتضح عند السامعين وصار حديثاً في الغابرين نحو الذين قدّمنا ذكرهم وغيرهم ممّن قال بمثل قولهم. فما استغنى من قبله عن ابن قتيبة ما ذكر أنه يغنيه إلا بالجهل كما استغنى هو به ورضيه وعادى العلم وأهله وكل امرئ عدوّ ما جهله.

تمّ الجزء الأوّل من ذات البيان. والحمد لله
رب العالمين وصلواته على رسوله سيدنا
محمد وآله الطيّبين الطاهرين صلوات الله عليهم أجمعين.
يتلوه الجزء الثاني: ذكر بيان قوله: والخراج بالضمان.

| الجزء الثاني من ذات البيان من تأليف القاضي النعمان بن محمد قدّس الله روحه ١٨أ
ورزقنا شفاعته وأنسه بحقّ سيّدنا محمد وآله الصادقين صلوات الله عليهم أجمعين.

| ذكر بيان قوله: ١٨ب
والخراج بالضمان

الخرج والخراج بمعنى واحد، وهو ما يؤخذ من الواجب المقطوع على من وجب عليه لمدّة معلومة، كما يؤخذ من أهل الخراج على أرضهم ومن العبد إذا قاطعه سيّده على شيء يؤدّيه من وقت إلى وقت.

وقد جاء هذا الحديث بلفظ مختلف وهو في معنى واحد. فرُويَ الخرج بالضمان والخراج بالضمان، وقد رُويَ هذا الحرف بالوجهين جميعا: ﴿فَهَلْ نَجْعَلُ لَكَ خَرْجًا﴾[١] و- نجعل لك خراجا.[٢]

وفي الحديث أيضًا: والغلة بالضمان،[٣] والغلة أجمع للقول وهو ما يُسْتَغَلّ من كرى الرباع والعبيد وغير ذلك.

---

[١] الكهف ١٨/٩٤.

[٢] راجع لهذه القراءة: الطبري، جامع البيان، ج ١٦ ص ٣٠.

[٣] ابن قدامة، المغني، ج ٤ ص ٢٣٩.

وبهذا اللفظ جاء الحديث عن أكثر من رواه عن رسول الله صلى الله عليه
وعلى آله أنّ رجلين اختصما إليه، اشترى أحدهما غلامًا للآخر فاستعمله
ثم وجد به عيبًا فقام به على بائعه منه وأراد ردّ الثمن عليه وردّ العبد البائع
١٩أ منه. فقضى رسول الله صلى الله عليه | وعلى آله بذلك، فقال البائع: يا
رسول الله إنه استعمله منذ زمان. فقال رسول الله صلى الله عليه وعلى آله:
الغلة بالضمان.[٤] وفي بعض الروايات:[٥] الخراج بالضمان، وفي بعضها: الخرج
بالضمان. ومعنى ذلك وبيانه أنّ ذلك يطيب للمشتري وأنّ السلعة تردّ بالعيب
لأنّها لو هلكت عنده لكانت في ماله فلمّا صار ضمانها عليه كانت غلتها له.

وهذا قول أهل البيت صلوات الله عليهم في كل ما يُشْتَرى فيوجد به عيب يجب الردّ به، أنّ للمشتري ردّه إذا لم يكن علم بالعيب ولا تبرّأ إليه منه البائع في حين عقدة البيع ولا استخدمه ولا انتفع به ولا عرضه للبيع بعد أن علم به. وإن كان شيء من ذلك فهو رضى من المشتري بالعيب ولا يجب له ردّه به. وقد وافق أهل البيت صلوات الله عليهم في الغلة أنّها تكون للمشتري بالضمان أكثرُ أهل الفتيا من العامّة.

---

[٤] قارن: أحمد بن حنبل، المسند، ج ٦ ص ٨٠.

[٥] أضيفت في هامش الأصل بنفس الخط.

وفرّق بعضهم بين ذلك فقال: إن كان حيواناً فولد وتناسل رُدّ وأولاده. وهذا لا يكون عند أهل | البيت صلوات الله عليهم وعند من وافقهم من العامّة إلا ١٩ ب
فيما كان من النتاج [في وقت البيع][٦] حملا وقد ولد. فأمّا ما حمل عند المشتري وولد فهو له، وإن ردّها وهي حوامل فالحمل للبائع المردود ذلك عليه بالعيب الموجود فيه، لأنّها لم يُظهرها ولم يُبيّن منها فيكون غلة، وإنّما هي زيادة فيها، وهي إذا زادت بصلاح أو نقصت من غير جناية المشتري للبائع على أيّ حال كانت من ذلك.

وقال فريق من العامّة: إذا اغتلّ لم يجب له الردّ بالعيب وله قيمته إذا كان ذلك في الحيوان، وما كان في الرباع فاستغله فله الغلة بالضمان، فخالفوا الحديث المرويّ عن رسول الله صلى الله عليه وعلى آله إذ[٧] جهلوه وقالوا بالرأي فيما فرّقوا بين البياعات فيه. وقد ذكرنا فيما تقدّم أنّ الواجب على من لم يعلم ما جاء من الأثر ولم يروه [أن يرجع][٨] إلى قول من | علمه ورواه. ٢٠ أ

فإن ادّعى البائع أنّ المشتري علم بالعيب قبل الشراء وأنّه أعلمه به، أو أنّه استخدم المبيع أو عرضه للبيع بعد أن علم العيب وأنكر ذلك المشتري وقام على البائع منه بردّ الثمن وصرف المبيع إليه فالبيّنة في ذلك على المدّعي،

[٦] ناقصة في الأصل واستدركناها من ف.
[٧] الأصل: اذا. وفي ف: إذ.
[٨] ناقصة في الأصل واستدركناها من ف.

وهو البائع، واليمين على المدّعى عليه، وهو المشتري، على سبيل ما ذكرناه في الباب الذي قبل هذا الباب من قوله: البيّنة على المدّعي واليمين على المدّعى عليه.

وبيان المدّعي من المدّعى عليه أنّ المدّعي هو من يطلب أن يأخذ شيئًا بدعواه أو يبطل بها ما وجب عليه، والمدّعى عليه هو من يُطلَب بما يؤخذ منه أو أن يُحَطّ عنه ما وجب له.[٩] فإن اشترى رجل جارية فوطأها ثم وجد بها عيبًا لم يكن له ردّها وله قيمة العيب، إلا أن يكون وجد[ها][١٠] حبلى فإنّه يردّها ويردّ معها نصف عشر قيمتها،[١١] كذلك جاء عن أهل البيت صلوات الله عليهم.

٢٠ ب | وإن أحدث المشتري حدثًا فيما اشتراه ثم اطلع على عيب فيه، فإن كان البائع قد علم ذلك العيب فكتمه ودلس على المشتري به، فللمشتري ردّ ما ابتاع من ذلك عليه ولا شيء عليه فيما أحدثه فيه، إذ لم يعلم بالعيب إلا بعد الحدث. وإن علمه ثمّ أحدث فيه شيئًا فقد لزمه وليس له أن يرجع على

---

[٩] أورد المحقق فيضي هذا النص من ف في حواشي تحقيقه لدعائم الإسلام. راجع: القاضي النعمان، دعائم الإسلام، ج ٢ ص ٥٢١.

[١٠] الأصل: وجد وفي ف: وجدها وهو أصحّ.

[١١] الكليني، الكافي، ج ٥ ص ٣١٤؛ القاضي النعمان، دعائم الإسلام، ج ٢ ص ٤٨.

البائع منه بشيء. وذلك أن يكون المبيع ثوبًا فقطعه أو نحو ذلك ممّا يحدثه المشتري فيما اشتراه أو يحدث عنده فيه، والقول بتصنيف ذلك يطول.

وإن قال البائع في وقت البيع للمشتري: أبيعك بالبراءة من كل عيب، وعقد البيع على ذلك، ثمّ وجد المشتري عيبًا، له الرجوع به. ولا يبرأ البائع إلا أن يُبيِّنَ العيب ولا يحلّ له أن يكتمه، وكتمان العيب من الغشّ. وقد جاء عن رسول الله صلى الله عليه وعلى آله أنه قال: من كان يؤمن بالله واليوم الآخر وباع بيعًا فيه عيب فَلْيُبَيِّنْهُ للمشتري و | لا يحلّ له أن يكتمه ولا لمن علم ذلك ٢١أ
غيره.[١٢] وقال: النصيحة واجبة لكلّ مسلم.[١٣] وقال: من غشّنا فليس منّا.[١٤] وبهذا قال أهل البيت صلوات الله عليهم، وكثير من العامّة قالوا فيه بقولهم.

وقال الآخرون من العامّة: إذا تبرّأ البائع إلى المشتري في حين عقده البيع من كل عيب فليس للمشتري القيام عليه بعيب إن وجده. وهم لا يجيزون بيع المجهول وما لا يعلمه المشتري، وهذا ممّا جهله ولم يعلمه.

---

[١٢] قارن: القاضي النعمان، دعائم الإسلام، ج ٢ ص ٤٧.

[١٣] لم نعثر على هذا الحديث بلفظه فيما بين أيدينا من مصادر. قارن المصدر السابق، ج ٢ ص ٤٧، حيث أورد القاضي النعمان الحديث بلفظ: الدين نصيحة.

[١٤] القاضي النعمان، دعائم الإسلام، ج ٢ ص ٤٧.

والعيوب تتفاوت ويفوق بعضها بعضًا . فلا يُجزى البراءة منها إلا بعد أن يراها المشتري ويقف عليها ، مع أنّ الذي جاء عن الأئمّة [من][١٥] أهل البيت صلوات الله عليهم في ذلك واجب قبوله إذ هو منقول فيهم عن رسول الله صلى الله عليه وعلى آله، وليس فيما جاء عنه وعنهم اعتراض. وقد ذكرنا الحجّة في ذلك عنهم فيما تقدّم.

وقال فريق من العامة: لا يُجزى البيع بالبراءة مجملا إذا كان البائع قد علم
٢١ب فيما باعه عيبًا حتى يبيّنه، وإن | لم يعلم وباع بالبراءة جاز ذلك وعليه اليمين.

وقال آخرون: يَتَبَرَّأ إذا تَبَرَّأ[١٦] من كل عيب إلا في الحيوان إن لم يبيّنه.

وقال آخرون: [يبرأ][١٧] من العيب إذا سمّاه وإن لم يره المشتري.

والقول ما تقدّم عن أهل البيت صلوات الله عليهم وقد ذكرت الحجّة فيه.

وقال قوم من العامّة في الأَمَة تُشتَرى فيطأها ثمّ يجد فيها عيبًا : إن كانت بكرًا ردّ عشر قيمتها وردّها ، وإن كانت ثيّبًا ردّ نصف عشر قيمتها وردّها إن شاء .

---

[١٥] ناقصة في المخطوطتين.

[١٦] الأصل: تبرئ. وفي ف: يبرأ.

[١٧] ناقصة في الأصل واستدركناها من ف.

وقال آخرون: يردّ معها حكومة، يعنون ما نقص من قيمتها.

وقال آخرون: يردّ معها شيئًا ولم يوقّتوا في ذلك توقيتا.

وقال آخرون: ليس له ردّها ويوضع عنه قيمة العيب.

وقال آخرون: يردّها ويردّ معها عشرة دنانير.

وقال آخرون: يردّها ويردّ معها مهر مثلها.

وقال آخرون: إن كانت ثيّبًا ردّها ولا شيء عليه[١٨] وإن كانت بكرًا ردّها ورجع بما نقصها من العيب من أصل الثمن.

وهذا كلّه | من قائليه رأي واستحسان منهم. وقد ذكرنا ما جاء في ذلك عن ٢٢أ
[الأئمّة من][١٩] أهل البيت صلوات الله عليهم ممّا هو مأخوذ عن رسول الله صلى الله عليه وعلى آله.

وإذا كانت السلعة [المبيعة][٢٠] أعدادًا من صنف واحد ومن أصناف شتى فيوجد العيب ببعضها، فإن كان ذلك ممّا له مثل فبدّله البائع للمشتري بمثله سالمًا من العيب، فليس له أكثر من ذلك. وإن لم يكن مثل يجري مجراه وكان العيب في وجه السلعة ومعظمها فإن للمشتري أن يردّها بذلك العيب بأجمعها. وإن كان ذلك في غير ذلك ممّا هو مجهول فيها وفي الدون منها لم

---

[١٨] الأصل: عليها. وفي ف: عليه وهو أصحّ.

[١٩] ناقصة في الأصل واستدركناها من ف.

[٢٠] ناقصة في الأصل واستدركناها من ف.

تردّ به وكان للمشتري قيمته. وهذا قول أهل البيت صلوات الله عليهم ووافقهم عليه فريق من العامّة.

وقال آخرون: يردّها كلّها أو يأخذها كلّها.

وقال آخرون: إنّ ذلك ممّا يرتبط بعضه ببعض، مثل أن يكونا نعلين أو خُفَّين
٢٢ب أو ما أشبه ذلك فيجد عيبًا فله أن يردّهما | جميعا. وإن باع أحدهما فليس [له][٢١] أن يردّ ما بقي ولا أن يرجع بقيمة عيبه. وإن كانا عبدين أو ما أشبه ذلك فوجد عيبًا بأحدهما، أخذ الذي لا عيب به بقيمة ذلك ممّا اشتراهما به وردّ الذي به عيب بقيمته كائنًا ما كان.

وإن كان الذي اشتُرِيَ حيوانًا أو شيئًا فعُطِبَ، و[به][٢٢] عيب لم يعلم به المشتري، فله الرجوع بقيمة العيب على البائع والمصيبة على المشتري كما تكون له الغلة. وكذلك إن كان عبدًا فأعتقه أو سلعة فوهبها أو تصدّق بها. وهذا قول أهل البيت صلوات الله عليهم ووافقهم عليه فريق من العامّة.

وقال آخرون: يرجع بقيمة العبد إذا دبر أو أُعْتِقَ أو وُلِدَ[٢٣] منه ولا يرجع به فيما باع أو وهب بعيب يكون فيه على البائع.

---

[٢١] ناقصة في الأصل واستدركناها من ف.

[٢٢] ناقصة في الأصل واستدركناها من ف.

[٢٣] في المخطوطتين: ولدت منه، ونرجّح أنّ ما أثبتناه هو الصحيح.

وإن اشترى عبدًا أو أمة فأبق من عند المشتري ثمّ علم أنه أبق قبل ذلك عند
البائع أو عند من باعه منه، فللمشتري الذي أبق | من عنده – إذا أثبت ٢٣ أ
البيّنة على أنه أبق من عنده – الرجوع بثمنه على البائع. ويطلبه البائع، فإن
وجده كان له إذ[٢٤] باعه وهو آبق ودلس بذلك وهو يعلم إباقه. فإن لم يعلم
بذلك فيما ذكر وحلف أنّه لم يعلم ولم تقم عليه بيّنة فللمشتري أن يأخذ بقيمة
عيب الإباق. ويطلب العبد، فإن وجده فهو له. وإن أخّر ذلك حتى يجده،
فإن شاء أن يردّه ويردّ معه قيمة ما نقص بالإباق الثاني وإن شاء أن يأخذه
بقيمة الإباق الأوّل، هذا إذا لم يثبت أنّ البائع علم بالإباق. فإن علمه ردّه
المشتري إذا وجده ولا يردّ معه شيئًا إن أحبّ ردّه. وهذا قول أهل البيت
صلوات الله عليهم ووافقهم عليه بعض العامّة.

وقال آخرون: لا يُقضى على البائع ما دام العبد آبقًا حتى يموت أو يوجد
ويردّه المشتري، وما نقص من الثمن فهو عيب يردّه به ما كان.

وإذا اشترى الجماعة السلعة | صفقة واحدة وهي ممّا ينقسم فقسموها ثم ٢٣ ب
وجد أحدهم عيبًا فيما صار إليه منها فله القيام به على البائع في قول أهل
البيت صلوات الله عليهم ووافقهم على ذلك بعض العامّة.

وقال آخرون: ليس له أن يردّ ذلك إلا أن يردّ الصفقة كلّها.

---

[٢٤] في المخطوطتين: إذا، ونرجّح أنّ ما أثبتناه هو الصحيح.

وإذا قام المشتري بعيب على البائع وجده فيما باع منه فقال البائع: إن شئت فخذ ما ابتعت بعيبه وإن شئت فردّه، فليس للمشتري إلا ذلك وليس له أن يأخذه بقيمة العيب[٢٥] شاء البائع ذلك أم أبى. وإن اتّفقا على أن يأخذ المشتري قيمة العيب فذلك جائز.

وهذه أصول ممّا تقدّم في الردّ بالعيب، ويتفرّع منها فروع كثيرة. فكلّ ما وجب ردّه ممّا ذكرناه من ذلك وما لم نذكره فليس على المشتري [شيء][٢٦] فيما انتفع به واغتلّ منه غير ما ذكرناه في بعض ذلك، وضمانه، إن هلك عليه، على الأصل الذي بدأنا بذكره من قول رسول الله صلى الله عليه وعلى آله: الخراج بالضمان.[٢٧]

٢٤ أ | وكذلك يجري حكم ذلك في سائر ما يدور بالأملاك مثل ما يُعاوَض[٢٨] به أو يُدفَع في حقّ وجب أو في صداق أو دية أو ما أشبه ذلك إذا وجد به عيبًا ردّه على من أعطاه ولم يكن على من أخذه فيما انتفع به أو اغتلّه منه شيء.

---

[٢٥] الأصل: يأخذ قيمة البيع، وأثبتنا النصّ من ف وهو أصحّ.

[٢٦] ناقصة في الأصل واستدركناها من ف.

[٢٧] الأصل: الخراج على الضمان، وأثبتنا النصّ من ف وهو أصحّ، ولم نعثر على هذا الحديث بلفظ: الخراج على الضمان.

[٢٨] الأصل: يعارض، وأثبتنا النصّ من ف وهو أصحّ.

وما لم يكن يُملَك بحقّ كالودائع وأموال الأطفال تكون في أيدي الأوصياء أو في يدي من توقف على يديه، إن تَجَرَ بها من هي في يديه فهلكت فهو لها ضامن ولا يطيب له ربحها. والوصيّ إذا تَجَرَ بمال اليتيم، فإن ربح فالربح لليتيم وإن خسر فالخسارة على الوصيّ أو على من كان [ذلك][٢٩] بيديه فتَجَرَ فيه.

وكذلك لا يحلّ أن يستخدم ما كان من ذلك من حيوان ولا ينتفع بشيء منه ولا يبيحه غيره، فإن فعل كان عليه أجر مثل ذلك وإن هلك فهو له ضامن.

هذا قول أهل البيت صلوات الله عليهم ووافقهم عليه أكثر العامّة.

ورخّص [بعضهم][٣٠] في ربح ذلك لمن تَجَرَ به لضمانه إيّاه.

وقال آخرون: لا يطيب له الربح ويتصدّق به.

و | قد قال الله عزّ وجلّ: ﴿لاَ تَأْكُلُواْ أَمْوَالَكُمْ بَيْنَكُمْ بِالْبَاطِلِ إِلاَّ أَن تَكُونَ ٢٤ ب
تِجَارَةً عَن تَرَاضٍ مِّنكُمْ﴾[٣١] وقال: ﴿وَلَا تَقْرَبُواْ مَالَ الْيَتِيمِ إِلَّا بِالَّتِي هِيَ أَحْسَنُ﴾.[٣٢] وقال رسول الله صلى الله عليه وعلى آله: كل ذي مال أحقّ

---

[٢٩] ناقصة في الأصل واستدركناها من ف.

[٣٠] ناقصة في الأصل واستدركناها من ف.

[٣١] البقرة ٢/١٨٨.

[٣٢] الأنعام ٦/١٥٢.

بماله.[٣٣] فمن تَجَرَ بما ليس له لم يحلّ ذلك له إلا عن تراض ممّن ذلك له إذا كان جائز الأمر، فإذا لم يكن ذلك فهو آثم متعدّ وصاحب المال أحقّ به وبما نما منه وطلع من الربح فيه. وإن هلك وكانت فيه خسارة فعلى المتعدّي فيه الضمان لقول رسول الله صلى الله عليه وعلى آله: كلّ يد لما جنت ضامنة.[٣٤] وما جرى ذكره من النمو والنتاج فيما يُباع فعلى ذلك يجري فيما يُمْلَك ويؤخذ بحقّ مثل الصداق والقرض وأشباه ذلك ممّا ذكرناه. ويجري مجرى البيع وما كان ممّا يؤخذ بغير حقّ كالذي ذكرناه ممّا يجري مجراه مثل السرق والغصب
٢٥ أ والخيانة والتعدّي | وأشباه ذلك. فضمان ما هلك أو نقص منه على المتعدّي فيه، وغلته وربح ما ربح فيه لصاحبه يرجع به وبما اغتلّ منه أو انتفع به على من تعدّى فيه. ولا يكون للمتعدّي من ذلك شيء بالضمان لأنّ الحديث، أعني الخراج بالضمان، إنّما جاء عن رسول الله صلى الله عليه وعلى آله فيما مُلِكَ بحقّ واجب. وما لم يُمْلَك بحقّ فسبيله ما ذكرناه من أنّه مال لمالكه وما اغتُلَّ منه وانتُفِعَ به فهو كذلك له.

وكذلك الرهن هو ملك الراهن وإنّما هو عند من ارتُهِن عنده وثيقة بحقّه، فإن هلك فهو من مال الراهن، وليس على من هو عنده رهنًا من ذلك شيء. وله

---

[٣٣] القاضي النعمان، دعائم الإسلام، ج ٢ ص ٤٨٨.

[٣٤] لم نعثر على هذا الحديث بلفظه فيما بين أيدينا من مصادر. قارن: ابن قدامة، المغني، ج ٦ ص ١٠٦.

أن يطلب الذي ارتهنه عنده بما هو رهن فيه إذا حلّ ذلك عليه وغلته ونفعه للراهن وليس للمرتهن من ذلك شيء.

وكذلك جاء في الحديث أنّ له غنمه وعليه غرمه.[٣٥] وإن هلك ولم يَجْنِ عليه الراهن فليس عليه أن يجعل مكانه عوضًا منه. فإن | جنى كان عليه ٢٥ ب
أن يجعل مكانه مثله. وسنذكر القول فيه بتمامه في بيان قوله: ولا يغلق [الرهن].[٣٦]

فهذا بيان ما لا يُستَغْنى عن بيانه[٣٧] من قوله: والخراج بالضمان، وقد ذكرنا أصوله. ويتفرّع من ذلك ما لو ذكرناه لطال ذكره. ولولا هذا البيان والوقوف على معرفته لم يدرِ من سمع الخراج بالضمان ما يوجب هذا اللفظ. ولو درى أنّ ذلك فيما بيّنّاه أوّلا أنّه قضى به رسول الله صلى الله عليه وعلى آله من ردّ السلعة بالعيب على البائع وأنّ للمشتري ما اغتلّ منها[٣٨] منذ اشتراها إلى وقت قيامه [بالعيب][٣٩] على بائعها منه، إذ هذا اللفظ في الحديث كما حكيناه، ولم يكن من سمع ذلك يعلم من البيان فيه ما ذكرناه لأُجْريَ ذلك في كلّ مبيع على[٤٠] كلّ حال ولم يجزه في غير البيع. وقد ذكرنا ما يجري حكم ذلك فيه.

---

[٣٥] الطوسي، الخلاف، ج ٣ ص ٢٥٧.

[٣٦] ناقصة في الأصل واستدركناها من ف.

[٣٧] الأصل: ما لا يستغنى عن قوله، وأثبتنا النصّ من ف وهو أصحّ.

[٣٨] الأصل: ما اغتلّ معناه، وأثبتنا النص من ف وهو الصحيح.

[٣٩] ناقصة في الأصل واستدركناها من ف.

[٤٠] الأصل: في كل مبيع ل كل حال، وأثبتنا النصّ من ف وهو أوضح.

٢٦ أ فمن أين يزعم ابن قتيبة أنّ ذلك يُغني عن تطويل[1] الفقهاء؟ | وما حمله على هذا القول إلا جهله بالفقه. فحمل من زعم أنّه أراد أن يبصّره وينبّهه على طلب العلم على الجهل الذي يكون من أجله من النقص [عليه][2] أضعاف ما ذكر أنّه تقيّد به، إذا لم يعلم من الفقه غير ما ذكره له وعرّفه أنّه يستغني به عن تطويل العلماء، إذ قد يأتي بذكر ذلك فإذا سئل عن معناه لم يدره ولا ما الحكم فيه، فكان بجهله أعذر منه بعلمه مع جهل حقيقته.

وبهذا ومثله يضلّ الضالون عباد الله عن الهدى. عصمنا الله من الحيرة والضلالة والجهالة بفضل رحمته وعزّته.

تمّ الجزء الثاني من ذات البيان والحمد لله ربّ العالمين.

يتلوه في الجزء الثالث:

ذكر بيان قوله: وجُرح العجماء جُبار.

---

[1] الأصل: طويل، وأثبتنا لفظ ف.

[2] ناقصة في الأصل واستدركناها من ف.

| الجزء الثالث من ذات البيان ٢٦ ب

من تأليف القاضي النعمان بن محمد

قدّس الله روحه ونوّر ضريحه

ورزقنا شفاعته وأنسه

بحقّ سيّدنا محمد وآله الطاهرين

صلوات الله عليهم أجمعين

بسم الله الرحمن الرحيم

ذكر بيان قوله:

وجُرح العَجماء جُبار

الحديث ثابت عن رسول الله صلى الله عليه وعلى آله أنّه قال: جُرح العَجماء جُبار.[١]

[١] راجع لهذه المسألة: الطوسي، الخلاف، ج ٥ ص ٥٠٩؛ الشافعي، إختلاف الحديث، ص ٥٥٦.

والعجماء كلّ دابّة أو بهيمة وجمعها الأعاجم. وقيل إنّها إنّما سُمِّيَتْ عجماء لأنها لا تتكلم، وكلّ ما لا يقدر على الكلام فهو أعجم. ومن ذلك قيل: صلاة النهار عجماء، لأنّ القراءة لا تعلن فيها.[٢]

والجُبار ما لا دية فيه وهو الهدر في لغة أهل تهامة.[٣]

وجاء عن رسول الله صلى الله عليه وعلى آله أنّ دابّة الرجل إذا أفلتت فأصابت إنساناً فقتلته أو جرحته أو أصابت ما أصابت من شيء فأتلفته أو أفسدته فليس على صاحبها في ذلك شيء. وفي هذا القول من النبيّ صلى الله عليه وعلى آله إنّه قال: جُرح العَجماء جُبار.

ووافق المنسوبون إلى الفقه من العامّة أهلَ البيت صلوات الله عليهم في ذلك

وقال جميعهم | فيه بقولهم ولم[٤] يخالفهم في ذلك أحد علمناه. ٢٧ ب

فإن أرسل الرجل دابّته أو ربطها في غير حقّه أو في طريق من طرق المسلمين فأصابت أحدًا فقتلته أو جرحته، أو شيئًا فأتلفته أو أفسدته

---

[٢] الشيخ الصدوق، معاني الأخبار، ص ٣٠٣. وعبارة القاضي النعمان هنا مطابقة حرفيا لعبارة الشيخ الصدوق.

[٣] لم أعثر فيما بين يدي من مصادر على تعليق القاضي النعمان في أنّ الجبار هو الهدر في لغة أهل تهامة.

[٤] في المخطوطتين: ولما.

فصاحبها ضامن لذلك في قول أهل البيت صلوات الله عليهم وقول النبيّ صلى اله عليه وعلى آله: جُرح العَجماء جُبار.

والعجماء جبار قول مجمل وهذا تفسيره، وإنّما يكون ذلك ما كان من فعل البهيمة ممّا لم يتعدّ فيه صاحبها، مثل أن تفلت على ما ذكرنا أو تكون في داره أو في موضع هو له فيدخل عليها داخل بغير إذن صاحبها فتصيبه أو تصيب شيئًا من ماله.

فإن كان دخل الداخل إلى القوم بإذنهم فأصابته دابّتهم أو عقره كلبهم ضمنوا ما أصابه. وإن دخل بغير إذنهم أو أفلت ذلك عليه فهذا لا ضمان فيه وهو جُبار كما قال رسول الله صلى الله عليه وعلى آله وأجمع المسلمون فيه كما وصفنا عنهم.

فأمّا ما ذكرناه من إطلاقه | إيّاها ووضعه لها في غير حقّه فإنّ ما فعلته في ٢٨ أ
ذلك فهو منسوب إليه وهو له ضامن لأنّ عليه حفظها في حيث يملكه ولا يكون ملكًا لغيره، إلا أن يكون قد أذن له فيه مالكه.

ووافق أهل البيت صلوات الله عليهم على هذا القول أكثرُ أهل الفتيا من العامّة.

وخالفهم بعضهم فقالوا: يضمن أهل الدار ما أصابه كلبهم أو دابّتهم إذا علموا أنها تصيب مثل ذلك، دخل الداخل إليهم بإذنهم أو بغير إذنهم وليس [لهم][٥] أن يمسكوا كلبًا عقورًا ولا بعيرًا مغتلمًا ولا دابّة عادية.

وقال آخرون: لا ضمان عليهم فيما كان في دارهم دخل من أصابه ذلك بإذنهم أم بغير إذنهم.

وقال آخرون فيما أفلت من البهائم والكلاب ممّا قد علم أصحابه أنه يعقر فأمسكوه: إنهم ضامنون لما أصاب وإن أفلت. وهذا خلاف ما جاء عن رسول الله صلى الله عليه وعلى آله.

وقد جاء عن أبي جعفر محمد بن عليّ [بن الحسين][٦] صلوات | الله عليه ٢٨ ب
أنّه قال: أتى رجل إلى رسول الله صلى الله عليه وعلى آله برجل فقال: يا رسول الله، إنّ ثور هذا قتل حماري. فقال له: ائتِ أبا بكر فاسأله وعُدْ إليّ بما يقول. فأتاه وسأله فقال: ليس على البهائم قود. فأتى النبيّ صلى الله عليه وعلى آله فأخبره.[٧] فقال: ائتِ عمر فاسأله وعُدْ إليّ بما يقول. فأتاه فسأله فقال مثل ما قال صاحبه. فرجع إلى النبيّ فأخبره فقال: ائتِ عليًّا فاسأله. فأتاه فسأله. فقال له عليّ عليه السلام: إن كان الثور هو الذي

---

[٥] ناقصة في الأصل واستدركاها من ف.

[٦] ناقصة في الأصل واستدركاها من ف.

[٧] الأصل: فأخبر، وفي ف: فأخبره وهو أصحّ.

دخل على الحمار في مأمنه حتى قتله فصاحبه ضامن، وإن كان الحمار هو الداخل على الثور في مأمنه فليس على صاحبه ضمان. فرجع إلى النبيّ صلى الله عليه وعلى آله فأخبره فقال: الحمد لله الذي جعل من أهل بيتي من يحكم حكم الأنبياء.[٨] وذلك أنّ هذا حُكم حَكَمَ به داود عليه السلام في مثل هذه القضيّة | بعينها.[٩] ٢٩ أ

وقال أبو عبد الله جعفر بن محمد صلوات الله عليه: بعث النبيّ صلى الله عليه وعلى آله عليًّا عليه السلام إلى اليمن يقضي بينهم. فأفلت فرس لرجل منهم فمرّ برجل فنفحه برجله فقتله. فجاء أولياء المقتول إلى عليّ عليه السلام بصاحب الفرس يستعدون عليه وأخبروه الخبر فأبطل دم صاحبهم وقال: إن أفلت فلا ضمان على صاحبه وإن أرسله أو ربطه في غير حقّه ضمن. فلم يرضَ اليمانيّون حكمه فأتوا رسول الله صلى الله عليه وعلى آله يتظلمون منه وقالوا: يا رسول الله إنّ عليًّا حكم علينا فظلمنا وأبطل دم صاحبنا. فأخبروه الخبر على وجهه. فقال رسول الله صلى الله عليه وعلى آله: إنّ عليًّا ليس بظلام ولم يُخلق للظلم والذي حكم به فيكم هو الحقّ، والولاية له من بعدي والحكم حكمه والقول قوله ولا يردّ حكمه وقوله إلا كافر

---

[٨] الكليني، الكافي، ج ٧ ص ٣٥٢.

[٩] القاضي النعمان، دعائم الإسلام، ج ٢ ص ٤٢٥ حيث نقل المحقق فيضي هذا النصّ من ذات البيان في حواشي تحقيقه.

ويرضى به المؤمنون. فلمّا سمع اليمانيّون من رسول الله صلى الله عليه وعلى آله | قالوا : يا رسول الله رضينا بحكمه وسلمنا لأمره. فقال رسول الله صلى ٢٩ ب
الله عليه وعلى آله فذلك منكم توبة.[١٠]

وسئل أبو عبد الله جعفر بن محمد صلوات الله عليه عن بختيّ مغتلم قتل رجلا فجاء أخو المقتول فقتل البختيّ، فقال: صاحب البختيّ ضامن لدية المقتول وعلى الأخ ثمن البختيّ، يعني إذا كان صاحب البختيّ أرسله أو أوقفه في غير حقّه.[١١]

وجاء عن النبيّ صلى الله عليه وعلى آله أنه قال: العجماء جبار والبئر جبار. يعني عليه السلام بالبئر هاهنا التي يحتفرها الرجل في حقّه فيسقط فيها الشيء فيعطب أو يموت، فلا شيء على صاحبها. وإن احتفرها في غير حقّه فعطب فيها شيء ضمن.

وفناء حائط الرجل من حقّه، فإن احتفر تحت حائطه بئر مرحاض أو ما أشبه ذلك لم يضمن ما هلك فيه. وإن حفر مثل ذلك في الطريق أو في غير حقّه ضمن ما هلك فيه.

---

[١٠] الشيخ الصدوق، الأمالي، ص ٤٣٠. وراجع: القاضي النعمان، دعائم الإسلام، ج ٢ ص ٤٢٦.

[١١] الكليني، الكافي، ج ٧ ص ٣٥١. القاضي النعمان، دعائم الإسلام، ج ٢ ص ٤٢٦.

ومن ذلك في قوله البئر جُبار، أنّ من احتفر بئرًا لآخَر فسقطت عليه فليس على صاحبها | شيء. ٣٠ أ

وجاء عن عليّ صلوات الله عليه أنه قضى في رجل دخل دار قوم بغير إذنهم فعقره كلبهم أنّه لا ضمان عليهم، وإن كان ذلك بإذنهم ضمنوا.[١٢]

وهذا بيان [قوله]:[١٣] وجُرح العجماء جُبار، وذلك فيما أصابت ممّا لم يتعدّ فيه صاحبها، وما تعدّى فيه فأصابته فليس بجُبار وذلك على نحو ما تقدّم ذكره وبيانه.

وكذلك إن رعت المواشي زرعًا أو شجرًا إذا أرسلها صاحبها فيه ضمن ما أفسدت منه. وإن أفلتت فيه من غير أن يرسلها نهارًا [لم يضمن].[١٤] وإن أفلتت ليلا ضمن، لأنّ على أصحاب الحوائط والزرع حياطة زرعهم وحوائطهم نهارًا وعلى أهل المواشي أن يحفظوها ليلا.[١٥]

وهذا الحكم هو الذي حكم به سليمان عليه السلام الذي حكاه الله عزّ وجلّ عنه بقوله ﴿وَدَاوُدَ وَسُلَيْمَانَ إِذْ يَحْكُمَانِ فِي الْحَرْثِ إِذْ نَفَشَتْ فِيهِ غَنَمُ الْقَوْمِ

---

[١٢] الكليني، الكافي، ج ٧ ص ٣٥٣.

[١٣] ناقصة في الأصل واستدركناها من ف.

[١٤] ناقصة في الأصل واستدركناها من ف.

[١٥] الكليني، الكافي، ج ٥ ص ٣٠١. الطوسي، الخلاف، ج ٥ ص ٥١١.

٣٠ب ﴿وَكُنَّا لِحُكْمِهِمْ شَاهِدِينَ﴾، الآية،[16] والنفش الرعي ليلا. فضمّن سليمان | عليه السلام صاحبَ الغنم ما أفلت فيه بالليل فرعته من الزرع.[17]

فلو حمل[18] قوله العجماء جُبار على كلّ شيء أفسدته أو استهلكته مَن سَمِعَ بهذا القول وعلمه ولم يعلم منه من شرح العلماء وتطويلهم ما ذكر ابن قتيبة أنه يُسْتَغنى عنه لكان بجهل ذلك الحكم[19] أعذر منه بأن لا يعلم حقيقة الحكم والوجه فيه.[20]

[16] الأنبياء ٧٨/٢١.

[17] الكليني، الكافي، ج ٥ ص ٣٠١. القمّي، تفسير، ج ٢ ص ٧٣.

[18] الأصل: حمل على، وأثبتنا النصّ من ف وهو أصحّ.

[19] أضيفت في الهامش بنفس الخط.

[20] الأصل: حقيقة الوجه فيه، وأثبتنا النصّ من ف وهو أصحّ.

ذكر بيان قوله:
ولا يَغْلَقُ الرهنُ

يُقال: غلق الرهن في يد المرتهن إذا لم يُفَكَّ، هكذا قال أصحاب اللغة. والحديث ثابت عن رسول الله صلى الله عليه وعلى آله أنه قال: لا يَغْلَقُ الرَّهْنُ، له غُنْمُهُ وعليه غُرْمُهُ،[٢١] يعني للذي ارتهنه.

وذلك مثل أن يرهن الرجل عند الرجل رهنًا في حقّ له عليه، ويشترط له أنّه إن لم يأته بحقّه إلى الأجل الذي بينهما، أنّ الرهن له بذلك الحقّ ولا شيء للراهن فيه، فهذا لا يجوز.

وكذا إن رهنه إلى أجل، فحلّ الأجل ولم يأته بما ارتهنه فيه، لم يملكه الذي هو في يديه | رهنًا، وهو رهن بحاله، وعلى الذي ارتهنه أن يؤدّي ما هو فيه رهنًا، وله أن يقبضه. وإن هلك فهو من ماله، والدَّيْن عليه بحاله. وإن زاد أو كانت غلة فذلك لصاحبه. ٣١ أ

[٢١] القاضي النعمان، دعائم الإسلام، ج ٢ ص ٨٣-٨٤ حيث نقل المحقق فيضي هذا النصّ من ذات البيان في حواشي تحقيقه.

وهذا معنى قوله: له غُنْمُهُ وعليه غُرْمُهُ، يعني أنّ زيادته وغلته [له]،[٢٢] وهلاكه من غير جناية الذي هو رهن في يديه، وغرم ما هو مرتهن فيه عليه، أعني على الذي ارتهنه، وزيادته له ونقصه عليه.

وهذا قول أهل البيت صلوات الله عليهم، ووافقهم عليه كثير من المنسوبين إلى الفتيا من العامّة.

وقال بعضهم: إذا رهنه على أنّه إن لم يأته بحقّه إلى أجل سمّاه كان الرهن له، لم يكن رهنًا وانفسخ ولا يكون بيعًا. وفي قول النبيّ صلى الله عليه وعلى آله: له غُنْمُهُ وعليه غُرْمُهُ ما أوجب أن يكون رهنًا. ولو لم يكن ذلك لم
٣١ ب يسمّه رهنًا، فيقول: لا يغلق الرهن، مع ما جاء في ذلك من بيان الأئمّة | عنه صلوات الله عليه وعليهم أجمعين.

فإن ارتهن الرجل رهنًا عند رجل وقال له: إن لم آتِكَ بحقّك إلى كذا فبِعْهُ واستَوْفِ حقّك، فما كان فيه بعد ذلك من فضل فهو لي، وما كان من نقص فعليّ، فإنّ ذلك لا يجوز. ولا يكون للذي عنده الرهن أن يبيعه لنفسه، إلا أن يرفع أمره إلى الحاكم فيأمر ببيعه. وإن جعلاه على يدي عدل على أن يبيعه العدل إذا حلّ الأجل، فذلك جائز.

---

[٢٢] ناقصة في الأصل واستدركناها من ف.

وهذا هو قول أهل البيت صلوات الله عليهم ووافقهم عليه كثير من المنسوبين إلى الفقه من العامّة.

وخالفهم آخرون منهم، فقال بعضهم: إذا جُعِلَ على يدي عدل فليس برهن.

وقال آخرون: للذي هو في يديه أن يبيعه إذا جعل ذلك الراهن له.

والقول ما قال أهل البيت صلوات الله عليهم إذ هو مرفوع إلى رسول الله صلى الله عليه وعلى آله، ولأنّ العدل بمنزلة وكيل للراهن والمرتهن، ولا يكون
٣٢ أ | المرتهن وكيلا على ما هو في يديه لغيره، وهو المطالب فيه. وهذا كلّه وغيره ممّا يدخل في معناه ممّا اختصرناه من أحكام الرهن [ممّا يدخل في قوله: ولا يغلق الرهن] .[٢٣]

وإذا لم يعلم ذلك مَن زعم ابن قتيبة أنّه يستغني بقوله: ولا يغلق الرهن عن مثل [هذا][٢٤] من تطويل الفقهاء، فأيّ شيء علم من ذلك؟ وهل هو إلا بمنزلة من جهل ذلك إذ لم يعلم منه إلا قوله: ولا يغلق الرهن، وهو لا يدري ما معنى ذلك ولا ما الحكم فيه؟

[٢٣] ناقصة في الأصل واستدركناها من ف.

[٢٤] ناقصة في الأصل واستدركناها من ف.

ذكر بيان قوله:
والمنحة مردودة

المنحة في اللغة ما أعطيته لينتفع به من أعطيته إيّاه. يُقال من ذلك: منح فلان فلاناً شاة يحتلبها. والمنحة الشاة نفسها، فإذا منحها المانح من يمنحه إيّاها ليحتلبها لم تكن له، وإنّما له منها [ما][43] أذنَ له فيه من لبنها لمدّة ما، يأذن له في ذلك وعليه ردّها إلى صاحبها. فذلك قوله والمنحة مردودة.

ويكون ذلك في كلّ شيء يُباح ليُنتفع به، أنّه لا يملك بذلك، وعلى الذي مُنِحَهُ | ردّه إلى المانح. وإنّما يكون له ما جعله له منه، كالدابّة يمنحه ٣٢ ب ركوبها، والدار يمنحه سكناها، والضيعة يمنحه ثمرها، والأرض يمنحه أن يزرعها، والعبد والأمة يمنحه خدمتهما.

ولا يجوز أنْ يمنحه وطء أمته لأنّ الوطء لا يحلّ إلا بنكاح أو بملك يمين لقول الله جلّ من قائل: ﴿وَالَّذِينَ هُمْ لِفُرُوجِهِمْ حَافِظُونَ. إِلاَّ عَلَى أَزْوَاجِهِمْ أَوْ مَا مَلَكَتْ أَيْمَانُهُمْ فَإِنَّهُمْ غَيْرُ مَلُومِينَ. فَمَنِ ابْتَغَى وَرَاءَ ذَلِكَ فَأُوْلَئِكَ هُمُ الْعَادُونَ﴾،[44] والفرج لا يحلّ لاثنين.

---

[43] ناقصة في الأصل واستدركناها من ف.

[44] المؤمن ٢٣/٥–٧.

فكلّ ما مُنِحَ من هذا فهو يُسَمّى منحة وردّه إلى أهله يجب، وليس لمن مُنِحَهُ إلا ما جُعِلَ له منها . قال ربيعة بن مُكَدَّم:[٤٥] (من الرجز)

قَدْ عَلِمَتْ إِذ مَنَحَتني فاها

أَنّي سَأَحْوي اليَوْمَ مَنْ حَواها[٤٦]

وإنّما مَنَحَتهُ من فيها أن يقبّله ولم تمنحه إيّاه.

وجاء عن رسول الله صلى الله عليه وعلى آله أنه قال: أتدرون أيّ الصدقة خير؟ قالوا : الله ورسوله أعلم. قال: خير | الصدقة المنحة.[٤٧] ٣٣ أ

والمنحة أن يمنح الرجل أخاه الدراهم، يعني السلف، أو يمنحه ظهر الدابّة، أو يمنحه لبن الشاة. وقال رسول الله صلى الله عليه وعلى آله: من منح منحة ورق[٤٨] أو سقى لبنًا كان له عدل نسمة أو رقبة.[٤٩] وقال رسول الله صلى الله عليه وعلى آله: أربعون خصلة لا يعمل عبد بخصلة منها رجاء ثوابها وتصديق موعودها[٥٠] إلا أدخله الله بها الجنّة، أعلاها منحة العنز.[٥١]

---

[٤٥] الأصل ربيعة بن مكرمة، وأثبتنا اسمه من ف وهو الصحيح. وهو ربيعة بن مُكَدَّم الفراسي الكناني، شاعر جاهليّ فارس شجاع. راجع عنه: الأصفهاني، الأغاني، ج ١٦ ص ٦٢.

[٤٦] المصدر السابق، ج ١٦ ص ٨٢.

[٤٧] الطوسي، المبسوط، ج ٣ ص ٣٠٣؛ المتقي الهندي، كنز العمال، ج ٦ ص ٤١٨.

[٤٨] الأصل: ورزق، وفي ف: ورق وهو الصحيح.

[٤٩] أبو عبيد، غريب الحديث، ج ١ ص ٢٩٣.

[٥٠] في المخطوطتين: موعدها.

[٥١] الحاكم النيسابوري، المستدرك، ج ٤ ص ٢٦٢.

وقوله: المنحة مردودة قول مجمل، وقد قدّمنا القول بردّها وأنّه[٥٢] لا يجب بما مُنِحَ منها حبسها. فإن هلكت من غير جناية من الممنوح عليها أو ضاعت، فليس عليه ردّها، وهي من مال [مَنْ][٥٣] منحها وله إذا وجدها.

وليس قوله إنها مردودة ممّا يوجب ردّها على كلّ الوجوه، إلا ما كان من الدراهم والدنانير ممّا يُمْنَح سلفًا، فإنّ ذلك يجب على من تسلفه ردّه، ضاع من يديه أو لم يضع. وليس يجري ذلك مجرى العاريّة، وسنذكر ذلك في موضعه. | وهذا كلّه قول أهل البيت صلوات الله عليهم. ٣٣ ب

[٥٢] الأصل: إنّما، وأثبتنا النصّ من ف وهو أصحّ.

[٥٣] ناقصة في الأصل واستدركناها من ف.

ذكر بيان قوله:
والعاريّة مؤدّاة

فالعاريّة ما يستعيره الناس بعضهم من بعض على أن ينتفعوا به ثمّ يردّوه إلى أهله، كالماعون والدواب والثمار والحلي وغير ذلك من الأمتعة والأشياء التي يُنْتَفَع بها. فإذا استعار المستعير[٥٤] العاريّة ممّن يعيره إيّاها فعليه ردّها. ومتى طلب صاحبها استرجاعها[٥٥] ممّن أعاره إيّاها وجب على المستعير ردّها إليه. فهذا معنى قوله: العاريّة مؤدّاة.

وذلك قول ثابت عن رسول الله صلى الله عليه وعلى آله، يعني [أنّه][٥٦] لا يجب للمستعير حبسها وأنّ عليه ردّها. فإن هلكت أو ضاعت من يدي المستعير قبل أن يردّها من غير أن يجني عليها أو يخالف ما استعارها [عليه]،[٥٧] ولم يكن ضمنها، فلا شيء عليه ولا يلزمه ردّها. وإن كان ضمنها لمّا استعارها فعليه ردّها أو ردّ مثلها أو قيمتها إن هلكت أو ضاعت عنده،

---

[٥٤] الأصل: المعير، وأثبتنا نص ف وهو أصحّ.

[٥٥] الأصل: ومتى طلبها صاحبها استرجعه الخ... وفي ف: ومتى طلبها صاحبها استرجعها الخ... ولعلّ ما أثبتناه هو الصحيح.

[٥٦] ناقصة في الأصل واستدركناها من ف.

[٥٧] ناقصة في الأصل واستدركناها من ف.

٣٤ أ جنى عليها أو لم يجنِ. وإن لم يكن | ضمنها وتعدّى عليها[٥٨] أو خالف ما استعارها عليه فيها، أو كانت دابّة فحمّلها فوق حملها، أو زاد في السير بها على الموضع الذي ذكر أنّه يريدها إليه، أو جنى عليها، أو ضيّعها، فهلكت أو ضاعت، فهو لها ضامن.

وقد جاء أنّ رسول الله صلى الله عليه وعلى آله استعار من صفوان بن أميّة[٥٩] مائة درع، [فقال له صفوان]:[٦٠] يا رسول الله، أمضمونة؟ قال: نعم.

وهذا كلّه قول أهل البيت صلوات الله عليهم، ووافقهم المنسوبون إلى الفتيا من العوامّ في أن لا يملكها المستعير وفي أنّه إذا جنى عليها ضمنها.

وخالفهم بعضهم في تضمينها.

وقال آخرون: ما كان من الحلي والثياب ونحو ذلك ممّا لا يظهر تلافه، فالمستعير له ضامن. وما كان من الحيوان والدور ممّا يظهر تلافه فلا ضمان فيه على المستعير.

---

[٥٨] الأصل: عليه، وأثبتنا نص ف وهو أصحّ.

[٥٩] صفوان بن أميّة بن خلف الجُمَحي، أبو وهب، المتوفّى ٤١ هـ. راجع عنه وعن الحادثة: الذهبي، سير، ج ٢ ص ٥٦٥–٥٦٦. وأوردها القاضي في دعائم الإسلام ج ٢ ص ٤٨٩.

[٦٠] ناقصة في الأصل واستدركناها من ف.

وقال آخرون بقول أهل البيت صلوات الله عليهم من أنّه لا يضمن منها إلا ما ضمن أو جنى عليه أو خالف المستعير ما استعاره [عليه].[٦١]

والدنانير والدراهم والفلوس لا تجري مجرى العاريّة لأنّها | إذا غابت لم تعرف ٣٤ ب
بعينها، وإنّما تجري مجرى القرض، وعلى من استقرضها ردّها.[٦٢]

[٦١] ناقصة في الأصل واستدركناها من ف.

[٦٢] أورد المحقق فيضي هذه العبارة الأخيرة من نصّ رسالة ذات البيان في حواشي تحقيقه لدعائم الإسلام. راجع: القاضي النعمان، دعائم الإسلام، ج ٢ ص ٤٨٩.

ذكر بيان قوله:
والزعيم غارم

هذا قول ثابت عن رسول الله صلى الله عليه وعلى آله، خطب به في حجّة الوداع فقال: إنّ الله [قد][٦٣] أعطى كلّ ذي حقّ حقّه، ولا وصيّة لوارث، والولد للفراش وللعاهر الحجر وحسابهم [على الله].[٦٤] من ادّعى إلى غير أبيه أو انتمى إلى غير مواليه فعليه لعنة الله [التّابعة][٦٥] إلى يوم القيامة. لا تنفق[٦٦] امرأة من بيتها شيئاً إلا بإذن زوجها. والعاريّة مؤدّاة والمنحة مردودة والدَين مُقتضىً والزعيم غارم. رواه الأئمّة من أهل بيت رسول الله صلى الله عليه وعلى الأئمّة من أهل بيته عنه.[٦٧] ورواه كذلك عامّة أهل الفتيا من العوامّ.[٦٨] والزعيم في لغة العرب هو الحميل يتحمّل الشيء عمّن هو عليه للذي هو له. ويقال له أيضا الكفيل والقبيل والصبير والضمين.[٦٩]

---

[٦٣] ناقصة في الأصل واستدركناها من ف.

[٦٤] ناقصة في الأصل واستدركناها من ف.

[٦٥] ناقصة في الأصل واستدركناها من ف.

[٦٦] كذا الأصل وفي ف: لا تنفقن. وقد ورد الحديث بهذا اللفظ أيضا. راجع: عبد الرزاق، المصنف، ج ٤ ص ١٤٨.

[٦٧] لم نعثر على هذه الخطبة برواية أئمّة أهل البيت عن النبّي فيما بين أيدينا من مصادر.

[٦٨] أخرج الترمذي هذا الحديث بلفظه كما هو هنا. راجع الترمذي، السنن، ج ٣ ص ٢٩٣. وقارن: أحمد بن حنبل، المسند، ج ٥ ص ٢٦٧.

[٦٩] القاضي النعمان، دعائم الإسلام، ج ٢ ص ٦٣.

وقد جاء عن رسول الله صلى الله عليه وعلى آله أنّه قال: أنا زعيم، | أي ٣٥ أ
الحميل، لمن آمن بي وهاجر ببيت في ربض الجنّة وببيت في وسط الجنّة، وأنا زعيم لمن أسلم وجاهد في سبيل الله ببيت في ربض الجنّة وببيت في وسط الجنّة وببيت في أعلى الجنّة. فمن فعل ذلك لم يدع للخير مطلبًا ولا من الشرّ مهربًا، يموت حيث شاء أن يموت.[٧٠] وقال عليّ صلوات الله عليه: أمّا بعد، فذمّتي رهينة وأنا به زعيم، في حديث كثير ذكره.[٧١]

وكذلك فسّر أهل التفسير قوله: ﴿وَلِمَن جَاء بِهِ حِمْلُ بَعِيرٍ وَأَنَاْ بِهِ زَعِيمٌ﴾[٧٢]. قال ابن عبّاس: كفيل.[٧٣] وقال قتادة في قوله: ﴿سَلْهُم أَيُّهُم بِذَلِكَ زَعِيمٌ﴾[٧٤]، قال: كفيل.[٧٥] [وكذلك][٧٦] قال أبو عبيد.

فإذا قال الرجل للرجل: ما لك على هذا الرجل فهو عليّ، فإن سمّى ما له عليه وقبل ذلك الذي هو له ممّن جعله على نفسه فهو له عليه. إن قام به

---

[٧٠] أخرجه البيهقي بلفظه عن محمد بن عبد الله بن عبد الحكم (ت ٢٦٨/٨٨٢) عن ابن وهب (ت ١٩٧/٨١٣) المصريين، راجع: البيهقي، السنن الكبرى، ج ٦ ص ٧٢.

[٧١] أخرج القاضي النعمان الخطبة بكاملها، راجع: القاضي النعمان، دعائم الإسلام، ج ١ ص ٩٧–٩٨. وقارن: اليعقوبي، تأريخ، ج ٢ ص ٢١١– ٢١٢.

[٧٢] يوسف ١٢/٧٢.

[٧٣] الطبري، جامع البيان، ج ١٣ ص ٢٦.

[٧٤] القلم ٦٨/٤٠.

[٧٥] الطبري، جامع البيان، ج ٢٩ ص ٤٦.

[٧٦] . ناقصة في الأصل واستدركاها من ف.

عليه وجب عليه غرمه كما جعله على نفسه [فهو له عليه]. [٧٧] وإن لم يكن ذكره وقام عليه بما يذكر أنّه له على المكفول عنه، وأنكر ذلك الكفيل، فعلى
٣٥ ب المدّعي البيّنة | فيما يدّعيه. فإذا ثبت ذلك وجب على الحميل غرمه له من ماله.

فإن كان حين تحمّل بذلك أمره المكفول عنه بأن يتحمّل به فيه، رجع بذلك عليه، إن كان ذلك بإقرار، بلا بيّنة. وإن لم يكن أمره بأن يتحمّل بذلك عنه لم يرجع عليه إلا أن تقوم بذلك بيّنة أنّه عليه. وإن شاء أن يستحلفه أنّ ذلك ليس عليه وأنّه ما أقرّ به ولا أمره أن يضمنه عنه فذلك له. فإن لم يحلف وحلف الضامن أن يضمن ذلك عنه رجع به عليه.

وإن كان صاحب الدَّيْن لمّا تحمّل به الحميل أبرأ الأوّل الذي عليه الدَّيْن، لم يكن له أن يقوم به عليه ويقوم بذلك على الحميل إن شاء، أو في تركته إن مات، أو في ماله إن غاب. وإن لم يكن أبرأه وقبل حمالة الحميل قام بماله على أيّهما أحبّ أن يقوم عليه من الحميل أو الغريم.

وإن كان إنّما تحمّل له بوجهه على أن يحضره إيّاه متى سأل إحضاره، كان
٣٦ أ عليه | أن يحضره له متى سأل، إلا أن يموت، أعني المكفول به. فإن مات لم يلزم الكفيل شيء ممّا تكفّل من إحضاره لأنّه قد هلك. وإن أنكر المكفول

---

[٧٧] ناقصة في الأصل واستدركناها من ف.

له موته فعلى الكفيل البيّنة [أنّه قد مات].[٧٨] وإن سأل استحلاف المكفول له أنّه لا يعلم موته كان ذلك له. فإن لم يحلف لم يقض له عليه بشيء حتى يحلف.

وإن غاب ولم يجده الذي تكفّل به فيحضره، كان عليه أن يؤدّي ما وجب عليه إلى من تكفّل له به.

وإن كفل الكفيل للمكفول له عن ميت بكفالة فقام بها عليه، فعليه غرمها. فإن أقرّ ورثة الميت بأنها على وليّهم، رجع بها الكفيل في تركته. وإن أنكروا ذلك وقامت البيّنة للكفيل بأنّ ذلك على الميت، رجع في تركته. وإن لم تكن له بيّنة كانت اليمين على[٧٩] الورثة أنّهم لا يعلمون ذلك ولا شيء منه على وليّهم المتوفى. وإن لم يكن الميت ترك شيئاً[٨٠] غرم الحميل ما تحمّل به إن قد سمّاه. وإن لم يُسمِّ ذلك | فالبيّنة على المكفول له كما ذكرنا أنّ ذلك ٣٦ ب
في الحيّ.

ولصاحب الدَّيْن أن يقوم به على الورثة في تركة وليّهم الذي دَيْنه عليه إن لم يبرأهم منه لمّا تكفّل به الكفيل أو على الكفيل أيّهما شاء.

[٧٨] ناقصة في الأصل واستدركناها من ف.
[٧٩] كتبت في هامش الأصل بنفس الخط.
[٨٠] الأصل: وإن لم تكن الميت ترك الخ... وأثبتنا النصّ من ف وهو أصحّ.

وإذا تكفّل الرجلان أو الجماعة لرجل بكفالة فله أن يأخذ بها أيّهم شاء، إلا أن بيّنوا حين تكفّلوا أنّه إنّما يلزم كلّ واحد منهم من ذلك بقدر حصّته. فإذا اختار المكفول له أن يأخذ بحقّه أحد الكفلاء، إن لم يكونوا بيّنوا ذلك، كان للمأخوذ بذلك، إذا وداه، أن يرجع على الباقين بحصصهم من الكفالة.

ولا تجوز الكفالة في القتل ولا في شيء من الحدود، أعني مَنْ اتّهم بذلك أو وجب عليه، لم يجب أن يتكفّل به ولا أن تُقْبَلَ كفالة فيه إذ لا يجب قتل الكفيل له إن غاب المكفول به. ومن شهد بذلك عليه ووجب النظر
٣٧ أ في الشهادة، أو اتّهم به أو لطخ عليه | فيه، فيجب حبسه إلى أن يتبيّن [أمره].[٨١]

وهذا كلّه قول أهل البيت صلوات الله عليهم ووافقهم عليه جماعة من المنسوبين إلى الفتيا من العوامّ وخالفهم في بعضه آخرون.

فقالت طائفة: إذا ضمن الضامن وقبل ضمانه من ضمن ذلك له، لم يكن له أن يرجع على المضمون عنه. ولم يذكروا في ذلك أبرأه أو لم يبرئه.

وقال آخرون: ليس له أن يرجع إليه وإن لم يبرئه، إلا أن يشترط أنّه يأخذ أيّهما شاء.

[٨١] ناقصة في الأصل واستدركناها من ف.

وقال آخرون: لا يرجع عليه وإن اشترط ذلك، إلا أنّهم قالوا: يُخَيَّر. فإن اختار أحدهما لم يرجع على الآخر.

وقال آخرون: إذا أحال الرجلُ الرجلَ بدين له عليه على مليء به وقبل الحوالة ثمّ أفلس المحال عليه، فليس لمن قبل الحوالة أن يرجع بها على الغريم.

وقال آخرون: لا يرجع عليه حتى يموت الذي أحيل عليه وإن أفلس، لأنّه لعلّه أن يجد ما صار عليه | بالحوالة. فإذا مات ولم يدع شيئًا رجع صاحب ٣٧ ب
الدين بذلك على غريمه.

وقال آخرون: إن أحاله على مفلس لم يرجع إلى المحيل إذا قبل الحوالة، وإن لم يعلم بأنّه مفلس فله الرجوع إلى غريمه.

وقال آخرون: إذا كفل الكفيل عن المكفول بما لم يُسَمِّهِ، وذلك أن يقول: كلّ ما لك على هذا فهو عليّ، ويقبل ذلك الكفيل، فإنّ[٨٢] الكفالة لا تثبت وليس على الكفيل شيء.

وقال آخرون: إذا تكفّل الرجل عن الرجل ولم يأمره بالكفالة عنه، فقام عليه من تكفّل له فأغرمه، لم يكن له أن يرجع على من كفل عنه بشيء.

وقال آخرون: له أن يرجع عليه.

---

[٨٢] في المخطوطتين: ان، ولعلّ ما أثبتناه هو الصحيح.

ولم أعلم أنّ أحدًا ممّن قال بهذين القولين بيّن إن كان الذي كفل به ثابتًا عليه أو غير ثابت، كما جاء عن أهل البيت صلوات الله عليهم أنّ ذلك إن ثبت
٣٨ أ على المكفول به ببيّنة رجع به من وداه عنه، لأنه حقّ لزمه وقد صار إلى | مستحقّه. وإن لم تقم له بيّنة لم يرجع عليه وعليه اليمين أنّ ذلك ليس عليه منه شيء.

وروى بعض أصحاب الشافعيّ عن ابن مسعود أنه قبل كفالة في حدّ. قال: ومن مذهب معلمنا، يعني الشافعيّ، أنّه لا يخالف الصحابيّ إذا لم يأتِ عن صحابيّ مثله ما يخالفه. قال: وفعل ابن مسعود ذلك بحضرة جماعة من الصحابة.[٨٣] فلزم من قال بذلك أن يجيز الحمالة في الحدود. وهذا قول قاله هذا القائل ولا أعلم أحدًا يجيز الحمالة في الحدود.

قال بعضهم: لا تجوز الحمالة بالنفس، يعنون حمالة الوجه. وقال بعض من أجازها أن المكفول بوجهه إن مات لزم الكفيل به ما كان يلزمه.

وقد قدّمت ذكر الواجب عند أهل البيت صلوات الله عليهم فيما ثبت عنهم بخلاف ما قال من ذكرت أنّه فارقهم من هؤلاء. وحذفت ذكرهم وما احتجّوا
٣٨ ب به فيما ذهبوا إليه، والحجّة عليهم فيه، اختصارًا لئلا أُطيل | الكتاب بذلك.

---

[٨٣] لم نعثر على هذه الأقوال المنسوبة للشافعي ولا على الحادثة المشار إليها فيما بين أيدينا من مصادر.

وسوف أثبت ذلك وغيره ممّا يأتي في أبواب الفتيا كلّها في كتاب الاتّفاق والافتراق إنشاء الله.

تمّ الجزء الثالث من ذات البيان

والحمد لله ربّ العالمين

وصلواته على رسوله سيّدنا محمد وآله الطيّبين الطاهرين

وسلم عليهم أجمعين.

يتلوه في الجزء الرابع

ذكر بيان قوله: لا وصيّة لوارث

الجزء الرابع من ذات البيان من تأليف

القاضي النعمان بن محمد قدّس الله روحه

ورزقنا شفاعته وأنسه بحقّ محمد وآله الطاهرين

صلوات الله عليهم أجمعين

| ذكر بيان قوله: ٣٩ أ

ولا وصيّة لوارث[١]

الوصيّة هي ما يوصي به الموصي في صحّته أو في مرضه بعد أن يكون صحيح العقل جائز الأمر فيقول: إن متّ فلفلان من مالي الذي أخلفه كذا ولفلان كذا ولفلان كذا وصيّة منّي لهم به، ويُتَصَدَّقُ عنّي بكذا ويُحَجُّ عنّي بكذا، ويُجْعَلُ مالي كذا وكذا في كذا وكذا لِما يذكره من أبواب البرّ، فذلك جائز بإجماع.

ويخرج عنه ما أوصى به أن يُخْرَجَ من تركته إذا كان الثلث منها فما دونه. وما جاوز الثلث من ذلك فلم يجز له إلا أن يجيزه الورثة الجائزو[٢] الأمر،

[١] راجع لهذه المسألة: القاضي النعمان، دعائم الإسلام، ج ٢ ص ٣٦٥.

[٢] الأصل: الجائزوا وفي ف: الجائزو.

فيجوز من ذلك على من أجازه بحصّته من ميراثه عنه قدر ما يجيزه. ومن لم يجز ذلك أو كان يولي عليه من الورثة، لم يجز عليه ما جاوز الثلث. وجاز من وصاياه ما يحتمل ثلث تركته فما دون الثلث. وفيما يعجز عن ذلك وما يبتدئ به من الوصايا إن عجز عن | الثلث كلام يطول به القول. ٣٩ ب

فهذا ما أجمع عليه الروّاة عن أهل البيت صلوات الله عليهم والمنسوبون إلى الفتيا من العوامّ كلّهم.

واستحبّ بعضهم الوصيّة بالثلث كاملا، واستحبّ آخرون أن يقتصر الموصي على ما دون الثلث وأن لا يجحف بالورثة. وأجمع كلّ من ذكرته أنّ الوصيّة للوارث لا تجوز، خلا شيء جاء عن بعض الروّاة عن أهل البيت صلوات الله عليهم سنذكره.

وقد روى أكثر الروّاة عنهم أن الوصيّة لا تجوز للوارث لأنّ الله [تعالى][٣] قد جعل لكلّ واحد من الورثة سهمًا [سمّاه الله][٤] له. فمن زاده على ذلك أو نقصه منه فقد خالف ما أمر الله عزّ وجلّ به. وذلك كرجل هلك فخلف ولدين ذكرين بعد أن أوصى لأحدهما بثلث تركته، فلو جاز ذلك لكان للموصى له الثلثان وللآخر الثلث. وقد جعل الله المال بينهما بالسواء.

---

[٣] ناقصة في الأصل واستدركناها من ف.

[٤] ناقصة في الأصل واستدركناها من ف.

وكذلك لو كانا ذكرًا وأنثى، فأوصى للأنثى الثلث، فلو جاز ذلك لصار لها
٤٠ أ أكثر | من النصف. وإنّما سمّى الله لها الثلث.

مع أنّ الحديث عن النبيّ صلى الله عليه وعلى آله ثابت صحيح أنّه قال: لا وصيّة لوارث، وهو على ذلك حديث مجمل لأنّه لو حُمِلَ على ظاهره لم تكن الوصيّة تجوز لوارث على حال من الأحوال ولا تحلّ له. وهي[٥] إذا أجازها باقي الورثة جازت له وحلت بإجماع، وإنّما المعنى في أنّها لا تجوز إذا لم يجزها سائر الورثة. ومن طاب نفسًا بحصّته منها للموصى له من الورثة جاز ذلك له، ويكون ذلك كالهبة والتسليم ممّن أجازه من الورثة وسلمه [له].[٦]

وهذا ومثله ممّا ذكرناه ونذكره من إغفال ابن قتيبة عنه إذ زعم أنّ ما ذكره من ذلك يُغني عن كثير من إطالة الفقهاء. وقد قال الله جلّ من قائل: ﴿كُتِبَ عَلَيْكُمْ إِذَا حَضَرَ أَحَدَكُمُ الْمَوْتُ إِن تَرَكَ خَيْرًا الْوَصِيَّةُ لِلْوَالِدَيْنِ وَالْأَقْرَبِينَ بِالْمَعْرُوفِ حَقًّا عَلَى الْمُتَّقِينَ﴾.[٧] وظاهر هذه الآية إذا سمعها من لم يعلم من
٤٠ ب تطويل الفقهاء ما زعم | ابن قتيبة أنّه يُسْتَغْنى عنه، رأى ذلك خلافًا[٨] لقول رسول الله صلى الله عليه و على آله: لا وصيّة لوارث. وقد أجمع كلّ من

[٥] الأصل: وهو، وأثبتنا النصّ من ف وهو أصحّ.
[٦] ناقصة في الأصل واستدركناها من ف.
[٧] البقرة ٢/١٨٠.
[٨] الأصل: راى ان ذلك خلافا، وأثبتنا النصّ من ف وهو أصحّ.

ذكرته ممّن يُذكَر بالعلم ويُنسَب إليه أنّ الوصيّة للوالدين اللذين لا يرثان، مثل أن يكونا مملوكين أو مشركين أو قاتلين للولد الموصي لهما أو على أيّ حال كانا لا يستحقان [شيئًا من][1] ميراثه، وللقرابة الذين لا يستحقون شيئًا من ميراثه ويحجبهم عنه من هو أقرب إليه منهم، جائز أن يوصي لهؤلاء وأنّهم يستحقون الوصيّة إذ ليسوا بوارثين. وقد ذهب بعض أهل التفسير من العامّة إلى أنّهم الذين عنى الله عزّ وجلّ بقوله هذا.

وقال آخرون: كان ذلك قبل نزول آية الفرائض. فلمّا نزلت وأعطى الله عزّ وجلّ كلّ ذي حقّ من القرابة حقّه، منع رسول الله صلى الله عليه وآله من أن يُزادوا على ذلك. واحتجّوا بقوله في الحديث ورووا أنّه خطب في حجّة
٤١ أ الوداع وهو على | ناقة فقال: إن الله أعطى كلّ ذي حقّ حقّه، ولا وصيّة لوارث، والولد للفراش وللعاهر الحجر وحسابهم على الله، ومن ادّعى إلى غير أبيه أو انتمى إلى غير مواليه رغبة عنهم فعليه لعنة الله والملائكة والناس أجمعين، لا يُقبَل منه صرف ولا عدل،[2] في كلام كثير خطب به يومئذ. قالوا: ففي قوله صلى الله عليه وعلى آله إنّ الله قد أعطى كلّ ذي حقّ حقه ولا وصيّة لوارث ما دلّ على أنّ ذلك إنّما كان قبل نزول الفرائض.[3]

---

[1] ناقصة في الأصل واستدركناها من ف.

[2] الطبراني، المعجم الكبير، ج ١٧ ص ٣٣.

[3] الأصل: على ان انما كان ذلك، وأثبتنا النصّ من ف وهو أصحّ.

فأمّا ما ذكرته من قول من نسب إلى أهل البيت صلوات الله عليهم أنّهم أجازوا الوصيّة للوارث فهي رواية شاذّة عنهم صلوات الله عليهم، والروايات الثابتة المتصلة المشهورة عنهم ما ذكرته ورووه عن رسول الله صلى الله عليه وعلى آله أنّه لا وصيّة لوارث.

وفي الرواية الشاذّة عنهم صلوات الله عليهم أنّ بعض الرواة زعم أنّ جعفر بن محمد صلوات الله عليه قال: لا بأس بـ﴿الْوَصِيَّةُ لِلْوَالِدَيْنِ وَالأَقْرَبِينَ بِالْمَعْرُوفِ حَقًّا عَلَى الْمُتَّقِينَ﴾.[١٢] وقول الله عزّ وجلّ: ﴿الْوَصِيَّةُ لِلْوَالِدَيْنِ وَالأَقْرَبِينَ بِالْمَعْرُوفِ حَقًّا عَلَى الْمُتَّقِينَ﴾ ليس ممّا يضادّ قول رسول الله صلى الله عليه وعلى آله: لا وصيّة لوارث، لأنّ الله عزّ وجلّ إنّما أباح الوصيّة لهم أجمعين بالمعروف ولا لبعضهم دون بعض، والمعروف ما أمر الله عزّ وجلّ به وفرضه. فمن وصّى[١٣] لهم بذلك جازت وصيّته ومن خالفه فقد تعدّى أمر الله سبحانه ولم يكن معروفًا ما فعله. وذلك كمن قسم ميراثه قبل وفاته على ورثته وأوصى أن يُصْرَفَ ذلك فيهم على ما سمّاه الله عزّ وجلّ لكلّ واحد منهم، أو

---

[١٢] البقرة ٢/١٨٥. وذكر القاضي النعمان هذه الرواية الشاذة عن جعفر بن محمد وأبدى رأيه فيها في دعائم الإسلام، ج ٢ ص ٣٥٨–٣٥٩.

[١٣] الأصل: وصيه، وأثبتنا النصّ من ف وهو أصحّ.

أن يوصي بالثلث فيما دونه للوالدين والأقربين الذين لا يرثونه[١٤] على ما قدّمنا ذكره، فذلك جائز.

فهذا بيان الآية والحديث، ولو كان في ذلك شبهة لما أجمع المسلمون عليه وقال جميعهم به والله أعلم.

---

[١٤] الأصل مضطرب وبيانه: "أو أن يوصي بالثلث فيما دونه وللوالدين والأقربين بالذين لا يرثونه". وأثبتنا النصّ من ف وهو أوضح.

ذكر بيان قوله:

ولا قطع | في ثمر[15] ولا كثر ٤٢ أ

قوله: ولا قطع في ثمر ولا كثر يعني: لا قطع على من سرق، أي لا يقطع يده إذا سرقه وإن سرق منه ما يجب القطع في مثل قيمته.

والثمر حمل الشجر، يقال منه أثمرت الشجرة فهي مثمرة. فمن سرق ثمرًا من شجر لم يُقطع. وكذلك إن سرق الشجرة أو النخلة بأسرها لم يُقطع.

والكثر الجمار، ومن سرقه أيضا لم يُقطع، لأنّ الحديث ثابت عن رسول الله صلى الله عليه وعلى آله أنّه قال: لا قطع في ثمر ولا في كثر. وإنّما يدرأ القطع عن سارق إذا سرقه من الشجر. وكذلك إنّما سمّي ثمرًا ما كان في شجره، فإذا قُطِفَ سُمّي كلّ شيء منه باسمه. ومن سرقه بعد ذلك وبعد أن يحرز قُطِعَ إذا بلغت قيمة[16] ما سرق منه ما يجب فيه القطع [وهو خمس دينار فما فوقه].[17]

---

[15] الأصل: ثمرة، وأثبتنا النصّ من ف وهو أصحّ. راجع: الكليني، الكافي، ج ٧ ص ٢٣٠–٢٣١.

[16] الأصل: قيمته، وأثبتنا النصّ من ف وهو أصحّ.

[17] القاضي النعمان، دعائم الإسلام، ج ٢ ص ٤٧٤ حيث أورد المحقق فيضي هذا النصّ من ذات البيان في حواشي تحقيقه. وقد أضاف فيضي في حاشيته عقب قوله: "ما يجب فيه القطع" عبارة: "وهو خمس دينار فما فوقه". وهذه العبارة الأخيرة غير مثبتة في ف التي نعتمدها.

هذا قول أهل البيت صلوات الله عليهم ووافقهم عليه جماعة من المنسوبين إلى الفتيا من العوامّ.

وخالفهم آخرون فقالوا: لا قطع في شيء من الفاكهة | والثمار وإن أحرز ٤٢ ب
ممّا يكون [لا][18] يبقى ويفسد إن بقي. وما كان منه يبقى ولا يفسد ففيه القطع.

وقال آخرون: يُقطع السارق إذا سرق الثمر من الشجر إذا كان [الشجر][19] في حرز حائط أو ما أشبهه، محيط بها.

وقال آخرون: من سرق ذلك يغرم قيمة ما أفسد ويعذر ولا يُقطع.

وقول رسول الله صلى الله عليه وعلى آله لا قطع في ثمر ولا كثر ممّا يوجب أن يدرأ به القطع عن سارقه إذا كان ثمرًا كما ذكرنا في شجره. فإذا جُمِعَ وصار في البيوت صار كسائر الأموال وسمّي منه باسمه وزال عنه اسم الثمر بالشجر، [وإنّما يلزمه اسم الثمر بالشجر][20] إذا كان فيها. قال الله عزّ وجل: ﴿ انظُرُوٓاْ إِلَىٰ ثَمَرِهِۦٓ إِذَآ أَثۡمَرَ وَيَنۡعِهِۦٓ ﴾.[21]

---

[18] ناقصة في الأصل واستدركناها من ف.

[19] ناقصة في الأصل واستدركناها من ف.

[20] ناقصة في الأصل واستدركناها من ف.

[21] الأنعام ٦/٩٩.

ذكر بيان قوله:
ولا قَوَد إلا بحديدة[٢٢]

القَوَد هاهنا هو دفع القاتل إلى أولياء المقتول والجارح إلى السجروح ليقتصّ منه. يُقال: أقاد السلطان من فلان وأقاد الرجل من نفسه. والاسم من ذلك
٤٣ أ القَوَد، شدّة | في العنق يمدّ معها الفرس رأسه، والإنسان كذلك والدواب، فلا يكاد يجمعه إلى صدره،[٢٣] يقال منه فرس أقود ورجل أقود،[٢٤] فكأنّه شبّه الذي يُقاد منه به.

وجاء عن رسول الله صلى الله عليه وعلى آله أنّه قال: لا قود إلا بحديدة. وهذا حديث ثابت عن رسول الله صلى الله عليه وعلى آله في قول أهل البيت صلوات الله عليهم،[٢٥] وكثير من العامّة أثبتوه وقالوا به.[٢٦]

---

[٢٢] في الأصل: إلا بحديد، وأثبتنا النصّ من ف وهو أصحّ.

[٢٣] لم نعثر على هذا التفسير اللغوي فيما بين أيدينا من مصادر. لعلّ القاضي يشير إلى ما يسمّى باللاتينيّة: torticollis أو strained neck.

[٢٤] في لسان العرب، مادة قود: والأقود من الرجال: الشديد العنق سمي بذلك لقلة التفاته.

[٢٥] أخرجه الدارقطني عن علي بن أبي طالب. راجع: الدارقطني، السنن، ج ٣ ص ٧٠–٧١.

[٢٦] ابن أبي شيبة، المصنّف، ج ٦ ص ٣٩٧.

ودفعه بعضهم وقالوا بخلافه وجاءوا بحديث احتجّوا به، والمعنى فيه أنّه إن قتل رجل رجلا أو جرحه بحجر أو بعصا أو بغير ذلك متعمّدًا فالقصاص من النفس.

ومن الموضحة فما دونها من الجراح ممّا يوصل إلى القصاص منه بلا زيادة ولا نقص، ويؤمن على المقتصّ منه[٢٧] التلف واجب عند أهل البيت صلوات الله عليهم ومن قال بقولهم.

ولا يُقتصّ من الفاعل إلا بحديدة | وإن كان فعله بغير حديدة. فإنّ [من][٢٨] قتل بحجر أو عصا أو حديدة، أو ما كان ممّا قتل مثل الوكز والخنق ودوس البطن وغير ذلك ممّا كان منه تعمّدًا، فمات منه المفعول ذلك به، قلّ ذلك الفعل أو كثر، صغر أو كبر، أُقيد من الفاعل، ذلك إذا قام عليه وليّ المقتول ودُفِعَ إليه ليقتصّ منه، وليس له، إن قتل وليّه بأيّ شيء قتله، أن يقتصّ منه إلا بالسيف يضرب به عنقه. ٤٣ ب

وكذلك جاء الحديث عن أهل البيت صلوات الله عليهم مرفوعًا عن رسول الله صلى الله عليه وعلى آله أنّه قال: لا قود إلا بالسيف.[٢٩]

---

[٢٧] الأصل: يؤمن منه على المقتصّ منه، وأثبتنا النصّ من ف وهو أوضح. راجع: القاضي النعمان، دعائم الإسلام، ج ٢ ص ٤٢٢.

[٢٨] ناقصة في الأصل واستدركناها من ف.

[٢٩] القاضي النعمان، دعائم الإسلام، ج ٢ ص ٤١٢.

وكذلك إن جرح رجل رجلا بما عسى أن يجرحه به فقام عليه وكان الجرح موضحة وما دونها ممّا يوصل، كما ذكرنا، إلى القصاص منه، بلا زيادة ولا نقص ويؤمن منه التلف، أستؤنِيَ بالجرح حتى يبرأ، وحُبسَ الجارح. فإن حدث من الجرح موت أو غيره ممّا يوجب قصاصًا أو دية حكم فيه بذلك.

٤٤ أ وإن برئ على غير عيب دُفِعَ | الجارح إلى المجروح، بعد أن كان قيس جرحه طوله وعمقه وعلّم له بالمداد على مثل موضعه من الجرح، ثمّ أخذ المقتصّ حديدة كالمبضع أو الموسى أو ما أشبه ذلك، فقيس منه مقدار ما كان عمق الجرح فغوّص له في عود وأخرج من الحديد بقدر ذلك القياس وسمّر عليه وأنزله المقتصّ في لحم المقتصّ منه حتى يبلغ العود وأجراه على قدر الخطّ بالمداد الذي خطّ عليه بمثل طول الجرح ثمّ رفعه، هذا إذا استوى لحم الجارح والمجروح.

فأمّا إن كان أحدهما أكثر لحمًا من الآخر،[٣٠] وكان الجرح موضحة، فللمقتصّ أن يبلغ العظم على ما كان جرحه، قلّ لحم المقتصّ منه أو كثر. وإن كان ما دون الموضحة لم يبلغ العظم. وإن انتهى قياس عمق الجرح إليه وما جاوز الموضحة، أو كان عظما، أو في مكان يُخاف على المقتصّ منه ٤٤ ب التلف، أو لا يوصل إلى حقيقة القصاص منه، لم | يكن فيه قصاص وكانت

[٣٠] الأصل: الاخرى وأثبتنا النصّ من ف وهو الصحيح.

[فيه][٣١] الدية ويعاقب الجاني السلطانُ على ذلك بقدر جرحه لئلا يتعدّى من يسهل عليه غرم الدية، فيفعل مثل ذلك [بغيره][٣٢] ممّن يريد أذاه وضرّه.

وإن كان القصاص من الأذن والأنف أو شيء زال من اللحم، أو طرف أنملة، عُلّم على مثله من المقتصّ منه وقُطِعَ بالموسى.

وإن كان من سنّ، قُلِع[٣٣] بآلة الحديد التي تُقلع بها الأسنان.

وإن كان من عين، رُبطت الصحيحة التي لا يُقتصّ منها وجميع وجه المقتصّ منه بخرق مبلولة، وأحميت مرآة حديدة حتى تحمرّ ثم تقدّم إلى عينه التي يقتصّ منها وتفتح حتى تسيل.

فبمثل هذا يكون القود من الجاني وإن كانت جنايته بخلافه، في قول أهل البيت صلوات الله عليهم وقول من وافقهم من العوامّ.

وخالفهم آخرون فيما يجب القصاص منه وفي كيفيّة القصاص. فزعموا أنّ يهوديًّا على عهد رسول الله صلى الله عليه وعلى آله | رضخ رأس امرأة ٤٥ أ
بين حجرين فماتت فأمر به فرضخ كذلك رأسه بين حجرين حتى مات.[٣٤]
واحتجّوا لذلك بقول الله جلّ ذكره: ﴿وَإِنْ عَاقَبْتُمْ فَعَاقِبُواْ بِمِثْلِ مَا عُوقِبْتُم

---

[٣١] ناقصة في الأصل واستدركناها من ف.

[٣٢] ناقصة في الأصل واستدركناها من ف.

[٣٣] الأصل: قطع، وأثبتنا النصّ من ف وهو أصحّ.

[٣٤] ابن أبي شيبة، المصنّف، ج ٦ ص ٣٦٥ و ٣٩١.

بِهِ﴾ [٣٥]. وهم يروون عن رسول الله صلى الله عليه وعلى آله أنّه قال يوم أُحُد لمّا رأى حمزة قد مُثِل به: لئن أظفرني الله بهم لأمثلنّ بسبعين رجلا منهم، فأنزل الله عزّ وجلّ: ﴿وَإِنْ عَاقَبْتُمْ فَعَاقِبُوا بِمِثْلِ مَا عُوقِبْتُم بِهِ وَلَئِن صَبَرْتُمْ لَهُوَ خَيْرٌ لِّلصَّابِرِينَ﴾ [٣٦]، وقال: ﴿وَاصْبِرْ وَمَا صَبْرُكَ إِلَّا بِاللَّهِ﴾ [٣٧]، قال رسول الله صلى الله عليه وعلى آله: أصبر يا رب، [٣٨] وأنّه صلى الله عليه وعلى آله نهى عن المثلة. [٣٩] وهذا ممّا يثبتونه من الأخبار عنه صلى الله عليه وعلى آله.

والعقوبة التي أباحها الله عزّ وجلّ في قتل النفس بغير حقّ قتل القاتل على ما وصفناه، وذلك قوله: ﴿النَّفْسَ بِالنَّفْسِ﴾ [٤٠]. فلو أنّ إنسانًا جرح آخر
٤٥ ب جراحات كثيرة مات منها المجروح أو خنقه أو ضربه بحجر أو | خشبه أو فعل به ما عسى أن يفعله لم يُقَد منه كما ذكرنا إلا بالسيف كما جاءت السنّة عن رسول الله صلى الله عليه وعلى آله بذلك، لأنّ النفس تأتي على كلّ

---

[٣٥] النحل ١٦/١٢٦.

[٣٦] النحل ١٦/١٢٦.

[٣٧] النحل ١٦/١٢٧.

[٣٨] القاضي النعمان، شرح الأخبار، ج ٣ ص ٢٣٠–٢٣١. قارن: السيوطي، الدر المنثور، ج ٤ ص ١٣٥.

[٣٩] القاضي النعمان، دعائم الإسلام، ج ٢ ص ٤١٢؛ المتقي الهندي، كنز العمال، ج ٤ ص ٣٩١.

[٤٠] المائدة ٥/٤٥.

شيء، وما كان دونها فهو اعتداء من فاعله.[٤١] وقد نهى الله عزّ وجلّ عنه في كتابه فقال: ﴿وَلاَ تَعْتَدُواْ إِنَّ اللَّهَ لاَ يُحِبُّ الْمُعْتَدِينَ﴾.[٤٢]

ومن زعم من العامّة أنّ القاتل يُقتَل بمثل ما قتل به فقد خالف السنّة ويُنكر قوله بذلك عليه، لأنّه إذا كان ذلك لم يكن للمقتصّ أن يفعل إلا مثل فعل الجاني لا يزيد عليه.

وقد يكون الجاني ضرب المقتول ضربة واحدة، فيجب على ذلك ألا يضربه الذي يقتصّ منه إلا ضربة واحدة، وقد لا يموت منها. أو يكون قتله إيّاه بفعل يفعل به مثله ولا يموت من ذلك الفعل من يقتصّ بمثله منه. وقد يكون مات المفعول ذلك به بأيسر شيء منه، فإن أطيل على المقتصّ منه، كان | اعتداء ٤٦ أ
وقد لا يموت منها. فهل ينبغي أن يُترك، ولا ينبغي إلا ذلك، أو قتله بغير اعتداء؟ وإنّما القصاص، كما ذكرنا، في النفس.

ولو أنّه تعدّى على إنسان فوطئه في دبره حتى مات، هل كانوا يوجبون أن يُقتصّ منه بمثل ذلك؟ وإن أوجبوه، فلم يطقه من له قصاص، أو فعله فلم يمت من ذلك المقتصّ منه، ما كان يكون الحكم فيه عندهم؟

---

[٤١] في المخطوطتين: من فعله، ولعلّ ما أثبتناه هو الصحيح.

[٤٢] البقرة ٢/١٩٠.

والقول في مثل هذا يطول والأعاليل فيه كثيرة مع ترك من قال به السنّة.

والثابت عن رسول الله صلى الله عليه وعلى آله، والأئمّة كذلك أيضا، ما ذكرته عن الأئمّة ومن وافقهم من العامّة[43] أنّه يُقتصّ من القاتل، إذا قتل،[44] بأيّ شيء كان إذا تعمّد ذلك.

فزعم بعض العامّة أنّه لا يُقاد من القاتل إلا أن يكون قد تعمّد ضرب المقتول بحديد محدّد مثل السيف والخنجر والسكين وبسنان الرمح وأشباه ذلك ممّا يشقّ بحدّه. قال: وما كان سوى ذلك فليس فيه قود وفيه الدية. وقال: لا
٤٦ ب يكون العمد الذي يوجب القود | إلا بحديدة.[45]

وقال آخرون: إذا ضربه[46] بالعصا والسوط الضرب الذي يكون الأغلب منه يقتل، أو شدخ رأسه بالحجر الثقيل والخشبة العظيمة أو ما أشبه ذلك ممّا الأغلب أنّ مثله يقتل، فمات من ذلك المفعول به، أقيد من الفاعل. وما كان دون ذلك وبغير حديدة فليس فيه قود.

---

[43] الأصل: من الأئمة، وفي ف: من الامة، ولعلّ ما أثبتناه هو الصحيح.

[44] الأصل: إذا قتل متعمّدا، وأثبتنا النصّ من ف وهو أصحّ.

[45] لعلّ القاضي النعمان يشير هنا إلى رأي الشافعي. راجع: كتاب الأم، ج ٦ ص ٦.

[46] الأصل: ضربته، وأثبتنا النصّ من ف وهو الصحيح.

وقال بعضهم: إذا بدأ وأعاد بالعصا فقتل، فعليه القود. وإن كان رماه بالحجر مرّات فمات فعليه القود، وإن كان ذلك مرّة واحدة فمات منها، فليس فيه قود.

[وقال بعضهم: إذا أغرقه في البحر فليس فيه قود].[٤٧]

وقال آخرون: إن غرّقه في شط بحر أو ما قد يكون يسلم ويعيش من غرق في مثله، فمات، لم يكن على من فعل ذلك به قود. وإن فعل ذلك فيما لا يُعاش من مثله، مثل أن يرميه في لجّة البحر أو ما أشبه ذلك، أو يثقله بشيء ويرميه في الماء، أو يمسكه فيه حتى يموت، أقيد منه بذلك.

وفرّقوا بين قتل العمد فقالوا: [هو العمد وشبه العمد].[٤٨] فالعمد هو القتل بالحديدة، وما ذكروه يجب القصاص | منه بغير الحديدة. وهو عند من قال ٤٧ أ بالقصاص به عمد، وعند من لم يرَ القصاص به وما هو دونه ممّا يتعمّده الفاعل، شبه العمد. وقالوا: عليه [فيه][٤٩] الدية مغلظة، وفي الخطأ الدية على العاقلة.

وإنّما ذكر الله عزّ وجلّ في كتابه العمد والخطأ. فأمّا شبه العمد فهو من رأي من قال بالرأي في دين الله جلّ ذكره. وليس في قول أهل البيت صلوات الله

---

[٤٧] هذه الفقرة ناقصة في الأصل واستدركناها من ف.

[٤٨] ناقصة في الأصل واستدركناها من ف.

[٤٩] ناقصة في الأصل واستدركناها من ف.

عليهم إلا العمد والخطأ . ووافقهم على ذلك كثير من العامّة غير ما ذكرت أنّه أوجب شبه العمد . فكلّ شيء تعمّد به الفاعل المفعول به فقتله به فهو عمد وفيه القود .

قال الله عزّ وجلّ: ﴿فَوَكَزَهُ مُوسَى فَقَضَى عَلَيْهِ﴾ ،[٥٠] يعني قتله بوكزة وهي الطعنة باليد .

وقد رُوِيَ عن عليّ صلوات الله عليه من طرق العامّة أنّه قال: كلّ عمد ففيه القود .[٥١] وذلك الثابت عنه وعن الأئمّة [من ولده][٥٢] صلوات الله عليهم والذي
٤٧ ب | آثروه عن رسول الله صلى الله عليه وعلى آله ونقلوه عنه من واحد إلى واحد ، وكذلك كل ما جاء عنهم وثبت من قولهم. فمن خالفه فقد خالف الله ورسوله وقامت بذلك عليه حجّته.

تمّ الجزء الرابع من ذات البيان والحمد لله ربّ العلمين.

يتلوه في الجزء الخامس

ذكر بيان قوله: والمرأة تعاقل الرجل إلى ثلث ديتها .

---

[٥٠] القصص ٢٨/١٥.

[٥١] لفظ حديث عليّ: العمد كله قود . راجع: ابن أبي شيبة، المصنّف، ج ٦ ص ٤٠٣ .

[٥٢] ناقصة في الأصل واستدركناها من ف.

الجزء الخامس من ذات البيان

من تأليف القاضي النعمان بن محمد

قدّس الله روحه ورزقنا شفاعته وأنسه

بحقّ سيّدنا محمد وآله الطاهرين

صلوات الله عليهم أجمعين.

| ذكر بيان قوله: والمرأة تعاقل الرجل إلى ثلث ديتها ٤٨ أ

قوله: والمرأة تعاقل الرجل، المعاقِلة الفاعِلة من العقل. والمفاعِلة لا تكون إلا من فاعلين تفاعلا، أي فعل كلّ واحد[١] منهما بالآخر، كما يُقال: تقاتل الرجلان وتضاربا وتشاتما إذا فعل ذلك كلّ واحد منهما بصاحبه.

والعقل هاهنا أصله من عقل البعير، وهو [أن][٢] تجمع يديه بعقال، وهو حبل تجمع به يديه أو تشدّ به ساقه وذراعه وتثنى ركبته فيبقى قائما على ثلاث قوائم. ثمّ استعير العقل للدية لأنهم كانوا يؤدّونها إبلا، يأتي بها من وجبت

[١] الأصل: كلّ واحدة، وأثبتنا النصّ من ف وهو الصحيح.

[٢] ناقصة في الأصل واستدركناها من ف.

عليه إلى من وجبت له، فيعقلها بفنائه إلى أن يشهد على دفعها إليه.[٣] فقالوا: عقل القتيل[٤] عقلا إذا وديت ديته. وكذلك الجريح، وعقل هذا الجريح كذا. وعقل فلان فلاناً إذا ودى ديته. قال أنس بن مدركة[٥] (من البسيط):

٤٨ ب | إنّي وقتلي سُلَيْكًا ثمّ أعقله.[٦]

فأراد بقوله: إنّ المرأة تعاقل الرجل إلى ثلث ديتها أنّه إن جرحها أو جرحته خطأً أو فيما لا يجب القصاص منه، أنّ دية جراحتها كدية جراحته سواء بحساب دية الرجل، حتى إذا بلغت قيمة جراحة المرأة ثلث الدية انحطت فرجعت إلى نصف دية الرجل، كما تكون دية المرأة في النفس نصف دية الرجل بإجماع من أهل الفتيا على ذلك.

فأمّا كمال أرش جراحها، ما دون ثلث الدية، وأنها تكون كجراحة الرجل وتعاقله كذلك إلى ثلث الدية، فهو قول أهل البيت صلوات الله عليهم الثابت عنهم، وإن جاء في بعض الروايات عنهم أنّ أرش جراح المرأة على النصف

---

[٣] القاضي النعمان، دعائم الإسلام، ج ٢ ص ٤١٤ حيث أورد المحقق فيضي هذا النص من ذات البيان في حواشي تحقيقه.

[٤] الأصل: عقل العقيل، وأثبتنا النصّ من ف وهو أصحّ.

[٥] أنس بن مدركة الخثعمي. راجع عنه وعن حادثة قتله سُلَيْكا وعقله في أخبار السُلَيْك بن السلكة: أبو الفرج الأصفهاني، كتاب الأغاني، ج ٢٠ ص ٣٩٧ – ٤٠١. وورد اسمه أيضا: أنس بن مدرك الخثعمي، راجع عنه: أبو عبيدة، الديباج، ص ٤٤–٤٦.

[٦] عجزه: كالثور يُضْرَب لمّا عافت البقر. أورد هذا البيت من الشعر الخليل بن أحمد وفسّره، راجع: الخليل بن أحمد، كتاب العين، ج ١ ص ١٦٠ (مادّة ع ق ل).

من أرش جراحة الرجل، فإنّ ذلك قول مجمل والمراد به فيما جاوز الثلث كما ذكرنا.

وبذلك كتب عليّ صلوات اله عليه إلى رفاعة:[٧] المرأة تعاقل الرجل إلى ثلث الدية.[٨] وجاء | عنه عليه السلام أنّه قال: أرش جراحة الرجل وجراحة المرأة ٤٩ أ
سواء حتى تبلغ ثلث الدية، فإذا كان ذلك رجعت إلى النصف.[٩] ورُويَ مثل هذا عن أبي جعفر محمد بن عليّ بن الحسين وأبي عبد اللّٰه جعفر بن محمد صلوات اللّٰه عليهما. وسئل أبو عبد اللّٰه جعفر بن محمد صلوات اللّٰه عليه عن رجل قطع إصبع امرأة، فقال: عليه عشر من الإبل؛ [قيل:][١٠] فإن قطع منها إصبعين، قال: عشرون من الإبل؛ قيل: فإن قطع ثلاث أصابع، قال: ثلاثون؛ [قيل:][١١] فإن قطع منها أربع أصابع، قال عشرون؛ قيل له: سبحان اللّٰه، لمّا عظمت مصيبتها قلّ أرشها، قال: بذاك جاءت السنّة، دية المرأة في النفس نصف دية الرجل وأرش جراحها ما لم يبلغ ثلث الدية على الكمال،

---

[٧] رفاعة بن شداد الفِتياني البجلي الكوفي، أبو عاصم (ت ٦٦ هـ)، راجع عنه: ابن حجر، تهذيب التهذيب ج ٣ ص ١٠٧. وكان رفاعة قاضي الأهواز لعليّ بن أبي طالب، راجع: القاضي النعمان، دعائم الإسلام، ج ٢ ص ١٧٦.

[٨] لم نعثر على كتاب عليّ هذا إلى رفاعة فيما بين أيدينا من مصادر.

[٩] لم نعثر على هذا الحديث المروي عن عليّ بلفظه فيما بين أيدينا من مصادر. وله شاهد عن جعفر الصادق، راجع: الكليني، الكافي، ج ٧ ص ٣٠٠.

[١٠] ناقصة في الأصل واستدركناها من ف.

[١١] ناقصة في الأصل واستدركناها من ف.

هي تعاقل الرجل إلى ثلث الدية فإذا جاوزت ثلث الدية رجعت جراحها إلى النصف.[١٢]

٤٩ ب فقوله: ثلث | الدية يعني الدية الكاملة، دية الرجل. وبيّن ذلك في أنّ لها في ثلاث أُصابع ثلاثين من الإبل وذلك قريب من ثلث الدية الكاملة، دية الرجل، لأنها مائة بعير ودية المرأة خمسون، وذلك على أهل الإبل. ودية الرجل من العين ألف دينار ودية المرأة خمسمائة، ذلك على أهل العين.

وفي قول ابن قتيبة المرأة تعاقل الرجل إلى ثلث ديتها وهم، ولو كان ذلك لانحطت في إصبعين لأنّ ثلث ديتها أقلّ من عشرين بعيرا.[١٣]

وقد وافق أهلَ البيت صلوات الله عليهم على هذا القول جماعة من المنسوبين إلى الفتيا من العامّة ورووا هذا الحديث: المرأة تعاقل الرجل إلى ثلث الدية عن زيد بن ثابت وعمر بن الخطاب،[١٤] ولا أعلم أحدًا منهم رفعه إلى النبيّ صلى الله عليه وعلى آله.[١٥]

---

[١٢] لم نعثر على هذا الحديث المروي عن جعفر الصادق بلفظه فيما بين أيدينا من مصادر. قارن: الكليني، الكافي، ج ٧ ص ٢٩٩.

[١٣] يريد القاضي النعمان بقوله هذا أنّ اللفظ إلى ثلث ديتها، كما ذكره ابن قتيبة، خطأ وأنّ اللفظ الصحيح هو: إلى ثلث الدية.

[١٤] الشافعي، كتاب الأمّ، ج ٧ ص ٣٢٩

[١٥] وفعلا، لم نعثر على هذا الحديث مرفوعا إلى النبيّ فيما بين أيدينا من مصادر. وهو يُروى أيضا عن سعيد بن المسيّب وعروة بن الزبير والحسن البصري. راجع: الحربي، غريب الحديث، ج ٣ ص ١٢٣٠.

فإن أراد ابن قتيبة أنّه من حديث الصحابة عند أصحابه فقد صدق، وإن أراد أنّه من حديث النبيّ صلى الله عليه وعلى آله فليس هو كذلك عند أصحابه. ولكنّه قال في الباب [الذي][١٦] ذكر فيه هذه الأخبار: ولا بدّ له من النظر في جمل الفقه و[معرفة][١٧] أصوله من حديث رسول الله صلى الله عليه وعلى آله وصحابته كقوله كذا، وذكر الأخبار. فلمّا قال: كقوله، كان ظاهر ذلك أنّه أراد قول النبيّ صلى الله عليه وعلى آله. ونسّق الأخبار على ذلك، فأضافها كلّها إلى النبيّ صلى الله عليه وعلى آله [ولم يذكر][١٨] شيئًا منها عن الصحابة الذين ذكرهم. وهذا من [سوء][١٩] توجيهه واستخفافه بما ينسبه إلى رسول الله صلى الله عليه وعلى آله، وهو يقول صلى الله عليه وعلى آله: من كذب عليّ متعمّدا فليتبوّأ مقعده في النار. فكان ينبغي له إذا ذكر أنّ الواجب النظر في جمل الفقه من حديث رسول الله وصحابته، ثمّ جاء بهذه | ٥٠ ب
الأخبار، أن يبيّن ما منها عنده من حديث الرسول صلى الله عليه وعلى آله وما منها من حديث الصحابة، ولا يقول كما قال: كقوله.[٢٠] وذلك في الظاهر

[١٦] ناقصة في الأصل واستدركناها من ف.
[١٧] ناقصة في الأصل وهي مثبتة في ف وفي أدب الكاتب.
[١٨] ناقصة في الأصل واستدركناها من ف.
[١٩] ناقصة في الأصل واستدركناها من ف.
[٢٠] يعني: كقول الرسول.

من قوله المراد به الرسول، ثمّ يأتي ببعض الأخبار ويقول: كنهيه في البيوع، ثمّ يأتي بباقيها فتصير كلّها على قوله مسندة عن رسول الله صلى الله عليه وعلى آله، وليس هي عنده ولا عند أصحابه كذلك.

ولكنّ هذا الحديث وما نذكره نحن عن أهل البيت صلوات الله عليهم فهو مسند كلّه إلى رسول الله صلى الله عليه وعلى آله، لأنّ قولهم كلّهم مسند عنه صلى الله عليه وعلى آله، لم يقولوا شيئًا منه برأيهم كما قال الجاهلون من العوامّ، لقول الصادق جعفر بن محمد عليه السلام: لنا من الحقّ مثل الذي كان لرسول الله صلى الله عليه وعلى آله إلا أنّا لا نحلّل ولا نحرّم إلا ما
٥١ أ أحلّه رسول | الله وحرّمه.[21]

وخالف أهلَ البيت صلوات الله عليهم في هذا القول الذي ذكرناه فريقٌ من العامّة وقالوا: دية جراحات النساء كلّها، ما قلّ منها وما كثر، على [النصف من دية جراحات][22] الرجال كما ذلك في النفس.

وقال آخرون: إنهما يستويان إلى نصف الدية [ثمّ تنحط المرأة إلى النصف].[23]

---

[21] لم نعثر على هذا الحديث المروي عن الصادق بلفظه فيما بين أيدينا من مصادر.

[22] ناقصة في الأصل واستدركناها من ف.

[23] ناقصة في الأصل واستدركناها من ف.

وقال آخرون: يستويان إلى المنقلة، والمنقلة هي الشجّة تهشم العظم فيسقط بعضه، أي يُنقَل منه. وفيها إذا كانت في الرأس العشر، ونصف العشر من الدية بإجماع مائة وخمسون دينارا وخمس عشرة من الإبل أو مثل ذلك مما سواها.

وقال [آخرون]:[٢٤] هما بالسواء إلى الموضحة في الرأس، وفيها نصف عشر الدية بإجماع أيضا.

هذا بيان قوله: والمرأة تعاقل الرجل إلى ثلث الدية.

[٢٤] ناقصة في الأصل واستدركناها من ف.

ذكر بيان قوله:
ولا تعقل العاقلة عمدًا ولا عبدًا ولا صلحًا ولا اعترافًا

قوله: ولا تعقل العاقلة، قد تقدّم في الباب الذي قبل هذا الباب بيان العقل
٥١ ب هاهنا ما هو. والعاقلة قرابة الجاني جناية الخطأ | يؤدّون عنه ما يلزم فيها.
وسُمّوا عاقلة لأنهم كانوا يأتون بما وجب في ذلك من الإبل [إلى][25] من وجبت له فيعقلونها بفنائه إلى أن يدفعوها [إليه][26] على نحو ما قدّمنا ذكره.
وإنّما يلزمهم من ذلك ما كان منه الخطأ ممّا يجاوز ثلث الدية بإجماع.

واختلفوا في الثلث وما دونه. والثابت عن أهل البيت صلوات الله عليهم أنّ العاقلة لا تؤدّي من جراح الخطأ إلا ما يبلغ أرشه ثلث الدية فصاعدًا، وما كان دون الثلث فهو في مال الجاني. ووافقهم على ذلك جماعة من المنسوبين إلى الفتيا من العامّة.

وقال آخرون منهم: على العاقلة ما جاوز الثلث، والثلث وما دونه على الجاني وليس على العاقلة منه شيء.

---

[25] ناقصة في الأصل واستدركاها من ف.

[26] ناقصة في الأصل واستدركاها من ف.

وقال آخرون: تعقل العاقلة الموضحة فما فوقها وما كان دون الموضحة فعلى الجاني. وقد ذكرت أنّ في الموضحة نصف عشر الدية. وقد جاءت مثل هذه الرواية عن أهل البيت صلوات الله عليهم، والرواية الأولى أثبت.

| وقال آخرون من العامّة: عقل الخطأ على العاقلة قلّ ذلك أو كثر. ٥٢ أ

وقال آخرون: تضمن العاقلة من الخطأ ما كان فيه غرّة عبد أو أمة.

فهذا اختلافهم في الوجه قد ذكرته والثابت منه.

وأمّا قوله: ولا تعقل العاقلة عمدًا ولا عبدًا ولا صلحًا ولا اعترافًا، فالعمد ما تعمّده الفاعل من قليل أو كثير فهو عليه في ماله بإجماع.

ومعنى قوله: ولا عبدًا، يعني ما جناه [العبد]،[٢٧] فهو في قيمته، إن شاء دفعه مولاه [في جنايته][٢٨] وإن شاء ودى عنه.

وكذلك إذا قتل [الحرّ][٢٩] عبدًا أو أمة خطأً أو جرحهما، فذلك في ماله وليس على عاقلتة شيء من ذلك.

والصلح ما ادّعاه الناس من الجنايات بعضهم على بعض، فمن ادّعى على رجل أنّه جرحه أو قتل وليّه خطأً ولا بيّنة له على ذلك وصالحه المدّعى عليه، فليس على عاقلته من ذلك الصلح شيء.

---

[٢٧] ناقصة في الأصل واستدركناها من ف.

[٢٨] ناقصة في الأصل واستدركناها من ف.

[٢٩] ناقصة في الأصل واستدركناها من ف.

وكذلك إن اعترف أنّه جرحه أو قتل وليّه خطأً ولم تقم على ذلك بيّنة
لم يلزم العاقلة من ذلك شيء، وكان ما يجب في | ذلك في مال المقرّ ٥٢ ب
المعترف [به].[30]

وهذا كلّه قول أهل البيت صلوات اله عليهم. وكتب عليّ صلوات الله عليه إلى رفاعة: لا تعقل العاقلة عمدًا ولا عبدًا ولا صلحًا ولا اعترافًا.[31] وعن عليّ بن الحسين صلوات الله عليه أنّه قال: إذا جنى العبد جناية خطأً فجنايته في ثمنه إن شاء سيّده فداه، وإن شاء سلّمه إلى من جنى عليه يسترقّه، وليس تعقل العاقلة عبدًا ولا امة.[32]

ووافق أهل البيت صلوات الله عليهم على هذا القول جماعة من المنسوبين إلى الفتيا من العامّة.

وفارقهم آخرون، فقالوا: تعقل العاقلة العبد والأمة إذا أصابهما الرجل خطأً.

وقال الآخرون في المعترف بجنايته خطأً: إنّ دية ذلك على معاقلته.

وقال آخرون: لا يكون ذلك [على العاقلة][33] إلا أن يكون المعترف مأمونًا.

---

[30] ناقصة في الأصل واستدركناها من ف.

[31] أورد القاضي النعمان هذا الحديث عن عليّ في دعائم الإسلام إلا أنه لم يذكر أنه في كتاب إلى رفاعة (ابن شدّاد قاضيه على الأهواز). راجع: القاضي النعمان، دعائم الإسلام، ج ٢ ص ٤١٦.

[32] لم نعثر على حديث عليّ بن الحسين بلفظه فيما بين أيدينا من مصادر. وراجع قول عليّ بن أبي طالب بلفظ متقارب: مالك بن أنس، المدوّنة الكبرى، ج ٦ ص ٣٦٧.

[33] ناقصة في الأصل واستدركناها من ف.

وقال آخرون: لا يلزم العاقلة ذلك إلا بلطخ وقسامة. ولم أعلم أحدًا أوجب في الصلح والمُتَّهَم مُنكِرٌ شيئًا.

وهذا الخبر، أعني | قوله لا تعقل العاقلة عمدًا ولا عبدًا ولا صلحًا ولا ٥٣ أ
اعترافًا، لم ترفعه العامّة إلى رسول الله صلى الله عليه وعلى آله، وإن رووه عن عليّ صلوات الله عليه وعن ابن عبّاس وعن الشعبي.[٣٤] ويدخل فيه على ابن قتيبة مثل ما ذكرنا أنّه يدخل في الخبر الذي قبله.

---

[٣٤] ورد هذا الحديث في المصادر السنّيّة موقوفا على الصحابة كعمر بن الخطاب وابن عبّاس والتّابعين كعامر الشعبي (ت ١١٠ هـ) وإبراهيم النخعي (ت ٩٤ هـ)، لكنّه ورد أيضا مرفوعا إلى النبيّ في مصادر أخرى. راجع: السرخسي، المبسوط، ج ٢٦ ص ٨٣.

ذكر بيان قوله:
ولا طلاق في إغلاق

وهذا حديث لم أسمعه من أهل البيت صلوات الله عليهم بهذا اللفظ ولكنّ معناه مأثور عنهم.[٣٥]

والعرب تقول: احتدّ فلان فنشب في حدّته وغلق، هذا قول الخليل بن أحمد، يريدون شدّة الغضب.[٣٦]

وجاء عن أهل البيت صلوات الله عليهم أنّ الطلاق لا يجوز إلا أن يكون للعدّة كما وصفه الله عزّ وجلّ في كتابه، أو للسنّة كما سنّه رسول الله صلى الله عليه وعلى آله. وهو أن ينوي الرجل طلاق امرأته ويقصده من غير غضب
٥٣ ب يعرض له فيبدر منه الطلاق فيه. وإنّهم صلوات الله عليهم لم يروا | الطلاق في سَوْرَة الغضب من غير قصد قبل ذلك [إليه][٣٧] واعتقاد له.

---

[٣٥] يعالج القاضي النعمان في دعائم الإسلام مسألة الطلاق بإسهاب بألفاظ قريبة لما في هذه الرسالة. راجع: القاضي النعمان، دعائم الإسلام، ج ٢ ص ٢٥٧–٢٦٠. وراجع أيضا ما أورده بألفاظ قريبة لما هاهنا: القاضي النعمان، الإقتصار، ص ١١٧–١١٨.

[٣٦] الخليل بن أحمد، كتاب العين، ج ٤ ص ٣٥٥ (مادّة غ ل ق). الجوهري، الصحاح، ج ٤ ص ١٣٥٨ (مادّة غ ل ق).

[٣٧] ناقصة في الأصل واستدركناها من ف.

فإن كانت المرأة مدخولا بها ممّن تحيض أمسك عنها ولم يقربها حتى تحيض وتطهر من حيضتها ، فيطلقها تطليقة واحدة ويشهد على ذلك شاهدَي عدل وهي طاهر في طهر لم يمسّها فيه. فإذا فعل ذلك فقد وقعت عليها تطليقة. ولو طلقها على هذه الصفة ثلاثاً أو ما زاد على الواحدة بلفظ واحد لم يقع عليها إلا تطليقة واحدة، وله أن يراجعها إن شاء وشاءت هي ذلك أوبته، ما لم تحِض بعد ذلك حيضتين. فإن تركها فلم يراجعها حتى حاضت حيضتين بعد ذلك فقد انقضت عدّتها بثلاث حيض وبانت منه وكانت أملك بنفسها. فإن رغب فيها فهو خاطب من الخطاب يتزوّجها إن شاء وشاءت بعقد مستأنف وتبقى عنده على تطليقتين. وإن كان راجعها وطلقها كذلك ثانية ثمّ راجعها | بقيت عنده على تطليقة واحدة. وإن طلقها كذلك ثلاثاً بانت منه ٥٤ أ
ولا تحلّ له إلا بعد زوج.

فهذا هو طلاق السنّة، أعني أن يطلقها تطليقة واحدة على ما وُصف، ثمّ يدعها حتى تنقضي عدّتها فتبين منه لأنّ له إذا فعل ذلك أن يراجعها إن شاء وشاءت، كما ذكرت، من غير أن تنكح زوجا غيره.

وطلاق العدّة أن يطلقها واحدة، كما ذكرت، ثمّ يراجعها ويواقعها ويدعها حتى تحيض وتطهر، ثمّ يطلقها ويشهد شاهدَي عدل على طلاقها. ثمّ يراجعها ويواقعها، فإذا حاضت وطهرت طلقها الثالثة كذلك وأشهد على

طلاقها. فإذا فعل ذلك بانت منه ولم تحلّ له إلا بعد زوج يتزوّجها تزويج غبطة بعد أن تطهر ويدخل بها ويطأها في الفرج، ويكون ذلك الزوج فحلا بالغًا. فإن طلقها أو مات عنها واعتدّت فشاء الزوج الأوّل وشاءت أن | ٥٤ ب يتراجعا [فذلك لهما][٣٨] بعقد مستأنف. وهذا هو الطلاق الذي أمر الله عزّ وجلّ في كتابه أن تُطَلَّق النساء به في قوله: ﴿يَا أَيُّهَا النَّبِيُّ إِذَا طَلَّقْتُمُ النِّسَاء فَطَلِّقُوهُنَّ لِعِدَّتِهِنَّ﴾، الآيات.[٣٩]

وإن كانت لا تحيض وقد دخل بها طلقها كذلك للشهور في رأس كلّ شهر تطليقة، واعتدّت بالشهور.

وأجمع الروّاة عن أهل البيت صلوات الله عليهم والمنسوبون إلى الفتيا من العوامّ أنّ هذا هو الطلاق الصحيح الجائز الذي أمر الله ورسوله من أراد الطلاق أن يطلق عليه، وأنّ من طلق ثلاثًا في مجلس واحد أو في غضب لم يقصد به حقيقة الطلاق، أو لم يُشْهِد على الطلاق، أو طلقها وهي حائض، أو في طهر قد مسّها فيه، فقد تعدّى حدود الله التي حدّها في الطلاق وعصى ربّه وخالف أمره، ولم يجز عند أهل البيت صلوات الله عليهم طلاقه ولا عند من وافقهم من العامّة.

---

[٣٨] ناقصة في الأصل واستدركناها من ف.

[٣٩] الطلاق ٦٥/١–٦.

[وقال غيرهم من العامّة][٤٠] وهم أكثرُ عددًا | أنّه، وإن خالف وعصى ٥٥ أ
وتعدّى، فإنّ الطلاق يقع ويلزم. وهم يقولون إنّه [إن][٤١] تعدّى وخالف في النكاح، لم يجز نكاحه. وهذا التعدّي الذي أجازوا معه الطلاق يبيح نكاح المرأة لغير المطلق، فصار النكاح عندهم جائزًا بالتعدّي والمخالفة. وقد أتوا ذلك وأباحوه[٤٢] من حيث جهلوا الواجب فيه.[٤٣] والقول في الحجج عليهم بذلك يطول ويخرج عن حدّ هذا الكتاب، وقد ذكرتها في غير كتاب ممّا بسطته.

فأمّا ما ذكره ابن قتيبة أنّ معنى الإغلاق الإكراه فذلك غير معروف في اللغة،[٤٤] ولا أعلم أحدًا احتجّ بمثله في طلاق المكره. والمُكرَه على الطلاق إذا أُكرِه عليه وخاف على نفسه فطلق لم يجز طلاقه في قول أهل البيت صلوات الله عليهم، لأنّ الله عزّ وجلّ قد أباح للمُكرَه الكفر[٤٥] إذا أُكرِه عليه ولم يعتقده

[٤٠] ناقصة في الأصل واستدركناها من ف.

[٤١] ناقصة في الأصل واستدركناها من ف.

[٤٢] الأصل: وأتوا ذلك واخوته، وأثبتنا النصّ من ف وهو الصواب

[٤٣] هذا اختصار لما أورده القاضي النعمان في دعائم الإسلام، ج ٢ ص ٢٦٤– ٢٦٥.

[٤٤] بل هو معروف ثابت في اللغة، وقد فسّر أبو عبيد القاسم بن سلام وابن قتيبة كلاهما الإغلاق بأنه الإكراه. راجع: ابن قدامة، المغني، ج ٨ ص ٢٦٠، حيث يورد المؤلف تفسيري أبي عبيد وابن قتيبة. وراجع أيضا: الشريف المرتضى، الانتصار، ص ٣٠٤، حيث يورد المؤلف تفسير أبي عبيد.

[٤٥] الأصل: اباح المكره الكفرة، وفي ف: اباح المكره الكفر، ونرجّح أنّ ما أثبتناه هو الصواب.

٥٥ ب بقلبه. وقال رسول الله صلى الله عليه وعلى آله: تجاوز الله عن أمّتي | خطأها ونسيانها وما أُكرهت عليه.[٤٦]

ووافق أهلَ البيت صلوات الله عليهم على ذلك فريقٌ من العامّة.

وقال آخرون منهم: يلزمه الطلاق وإن أُكرِه عليه.

وقال آخرون منهم: إن كان السلطان هو الذي أكرهه جاز طلاقه، وإن أكرهه على ذلك لصوص لم يجز طلاقه.

فعلى هذا الذي ذكرته، ذكرته عن أهل البيت صلوات الله عليهم ومن وافقهم: لا يجوز الطلاق في غضب ولا يجوز إلا على ما وصفته ممّا أمر الله عزّ وجلّ ورسوله صلى الله عليه وعلى آله.

فهذا بيان قوله: لا طلاق في إغلاق.

---

[٤٦] الحاكم النيسابوري، المستدرك، ج ٢ ص ١٩٨.

ذكر بيان قوله:
والبَيِّعانِ بالخيار ما لم يفترقا

البيّعان عنى بذلك البائع والمشتري، كذلك قال الخليل بن أحمد، قال: والعرب تقول بعت في معنى اشتريت ولا تبع بمعنى لا تشتر.[٤٧]

وهذا حديث [ثابت][٤٨] عن النبيّ صلى الله عليه وعلى آله أنّه قال: البيّعان بالخيار ما لم يفترقا، رواه الأئمّة | من أهل بيت رسول الله صلى الله عليه ٥٦ أ
وعليهم السلام والمنسوبون إلى الفتيا من العوامّ.

وفي بعض الروايات: البيّعان بالخيار ما لم يفترقا إلا بيع خيار،[٤٩] يعني أنّ كلّ واحد منهما بالخيار إن شاء فسخه ورجع[٥٠] عنه ما لم يفترقا عن إيجاب له. وقوله إلا بيع خيار مستثنى من ذلك، وهو أن يعقد البيع على أنّ لهما أو لأحدهما الخيار في ذلك البيع إلى مدّة معلومة أو إلى غير مدّة، فلا يكون حينئذ افتراقهما موجبا للبيع ما لم تنقض تلك المدّة التي جعلا الخيار إليها.

---

[٤٧] الخليل بن أحمد، كتاب العين، ج ٢ ص ٢٦٥، باب ب ي ع.

[٤٨] ناقصة في الأصل واستدركناها من ف.

[٤٩] ورد هذا الحديث بلفظ: البيّعان بالخيار ما لم يفترقا، أو يكون بيع خيار. راجع: عبد الرزّاق، المصنّف، ج ٨ ص ٥١.

[٥٠] الأصل: ويرجع، وأثبتنا النصّ من ف وهو أصحّ.

ولمن جعل ذلك له أن يرجع بما اشترطه بينه وبين تلك المدّة. فإذا انقضت لم يكن له الرجوع ومضى البيع كانت المدّة في ذلك ما كانت. وإن لم يوقتا لذلك مدّة فالخيار لمن جعل [له][٥١] ومتى قام فيه، وذلك لقول رسول الله صلى الله عليه وعلى آله: المسلون عند شروطهم ما لم يُخالَف كتاب الله، ومن شرط
شرطًا يخالف | كتاب الله فشرطه باطل.[٥٢] ٥٦ ب

هذا قول أهل البيت صلوات الله عليهم ووافقهم عليه جماعة من المنسوبين إلى أهل الفتيا من العامّة.

وخالفهم آخرون فقالوا: لا يجوز من الشرط إلا ما كانت مدّته ثلاثة أيّام فما دونها، وما جاوز ثلاثة أيّام لم يجز.

وقال بعضهم: إذا عُقِد البيع على شرط تجاوز ثلاثة أيّام فسد البيع والشرط.

وقال آخرون: البيع جائز والشرط باطل.

وفرّقت فرقة ثالثة في ذلك بين السلع، فقالت: يجوز في الثوب ونحوه الخيار اليوم واليومين، وفي الرقيق مثل الخمسة الأيّام والجمعة ونحو ذلك، وفي

---

[٥١] ناقصة في الأصل واستدركناها من ف.

[٥٢] الطوسي، تهذيب الأحكام، ج ٧ ص ٢٢. قارن: عبد الرزاق، المصنف، ج ٩ ص ٨. وراجع: القاضي النعمان، دعائم الإسلام، ج ٢ ص ٤٣، حيث ينقل المحقق فيضي في حواشي تحقيقه هذا النصّ من ذات البيان إلى قوله: فشرطه باطل.

الدار الشهر وما أشبهه، ولا يجوز الخيار إلى أكثر من ذلك. وهذا رأي ممّن قال به.

واختلفوا بعد اجتماعهم على صحّة الحديث، أنّ رسول الله صلى الله عليه وعلى آله قال: البيّعان بالخيار ما لم يفترقا، في صفة الفرقة. قال قوم: هي أن يفترقا بالأبدان من الموضع الذي عُقِدَ [فيه][٥٣] البيع | فإذا افترقا منه بعد أن ٥٧ أ
عُقِد البيع لم يكن لأحد منهما فيه خيار إذا لم يُشترط الخيار.

هذا قول أهل البيت صلوات الله عليهم ووافقهم عليه جماعة من المنسوبين إلى الفتيا من العامّة. وجاء عن أبي جعفر محمد بن عليّ بن الحسين وأبي عبد الله جعفر بن محمد صلوات الله عليهما أنّهما ابتاعا بيعًا فقام كل واحد منهما لما عُقد البيع فمشى حتى فارق البائع منه وقال: أردت بهذا أن يجب البيع.[٥٤]

وفارقهم آخرون من العامّة فقالوا: معنى الافتراق وجوب البيع بين المتبايعَين، وهذا تَقَوّل منهم، والافتراق المعروف في لغة العرب هو ما ذكرناه. وفي هذا وغيره ممّا ذكرناه ونذكره في هذا الكتاب وسائر الفتيا احتجاج كثير حذفناه مع

---

[٥٣] ناقصة في الأصل واستدركناها من ف.

[٥٤] الكليني، الكافي، ج ١٧٠–١٧١.

ذكر القائلين بذلك اختصارًا لئلا يطول الكتاب به. وأثبتنا ذلك كلّه في كتاب الاتفاق والافتراق، فمن آثر علم ذلك طلبه فيه فوجده إن شاء الله تعالى.

تمّ الجزء الخامس من ذات البيان والحمد لله ربّ العلمين.

يتلوه في الجزء السادس

ذكر بيان قوله: الجار أحقّ بصقبه.

الجزء السادس من ذات البيان

من تأليف القاضي النعمان بن محمد

قدّس الله روحه ورزقنا شفاعته وأنسه

بحقّ سيّدنا محمد وآله الطيّبين الطاهرين

صلوات الله عليهم أجمعين

٥٨ أ | بسم الله الرحمن الرحيم

ذكر بيان قوله:

الجار أحقّ بِصَقَبِهِ

هذا قول قال بعض أهل الحديث إنّه روي عن رسول الله صلى الله عليه وعلى آله ودفعه آخرون، وسنذكر قول من قال به ومن دفعه.

والجار في اللغة الذي يجاورك في السكن، والجار الذي استجارك لتجيره وتمنعه ويكون في ذمّتك، والجار من يكون في المحلة أو المدينة، كما روي عن علي صلوات الله عليه أنّه قال: لا صلاة لجار المسجد إلا في المسجد،

فقيل له: ومن جار المسجد؟ قال: من سمع النداء،[١] يعني، لا صلاة كصلاة الجماعة.[٢] وقد ذكرت القول في هذا[٣] بتمامه في كثير ممّا بسطته من الفقه في أبواب المساجد.[٤]

وقد قال بعض المنسوبين إلى الفقه من العامّة: يقع اسم الجار على من بينك وبينه أربعون دارًا[٥] فما دونها. والجار من قرب منك وكان بجانبك.

٥٨ ب | وقد قال الشافعي: فإن قال قائل: فهل تسمّي العرب الشريك جارًا؟ قلنا: نعم، كلّ من قرب بدنه بدن صاحبه فهو جار له. واستشهد بحديث حمل بن مالك بن النابغة: كنت بين جارتين[٦] لي، فضربت إحداهما الأخرى بمسطح

[١] راجع: القاضي النعمان، دعائم الإسلام، ج ١ ص١٤٨؛ الشافعي، كتاب الأمّ، ج ٧ ص ١٧٤؛ عبد الرزاق، المصنّف، ج ١ ص ٤٩٧ – ٤٩٨.

[٢] في المخطوطتين: لا صلاة فضل كصلاة الجماعة، ورجّحنا أنّ كلمة «فضل» زائدة، أو تكون العبارة: لا صلاة أفضل من صلاة الجماعة.

[٣] الأصل: ذكرت هذا القول في هذا، وأثبتنا النصّ من ف وهو أصحّ.

[٤] القاضي النعمان، دعائم الإسلام، ج ١ ص ١٤٨. القاضي النعمان، الاقتصار، ص ٢٣.

[٥] الأصل: أربعون ذراعا، وأثبتنا النصّ من ف تبعا لما ذكره الشافعي. راجع: الشافعي، كتاب الأم، ج ٧ ص ١١٧.

[٦] الأصل: جاريتين، وأثبتنا النصّ من ف تبعا لما ذكره الشافعي في المرجع المذكور أعلاه.

فألقت جنينا ميتا، فقضى فيه رسول الله بغرّة.[٧] والعرب تسمّي الزوجة جارًا لقربها من الرجل. [قال الأعشى][٨] (من الطويل):

أجارتنا بيني فإنّك طالقه.[٩]

فالجوار في اللغة يقع على البعد والقرب عمومًا.[١٠]

فإذا حصل ذلك على الخصوص كان على الأقرب فالأقرب، كما يقول الرجل لمن هو معه في مدينة إذا كان معه غيره من غيرها: هذا جاري دونك. وإن كان في محلة مع غيره ممن بعد عنه من أهل المدينة التي هو فيها، كان صاحب المحلة أحقّ بأن يقال له ذلك، وكذلك الأقرب فالأقرب. ومن ذلك قول | عائشة لرسول الله صلى الله عليه وعلى آله: لي جاران، بأيّهما أبدأ؟ ٥٩ أ
قال: بأقربهما بابًا.[١١]

ذكرت معنى الجار لما في هذا القول من الحكم الذي يحتاج إلى ذكر ذلك وبيانه فيه.

---

[٧] نقل القاضي النعمان هذه الفقرة حرفيًا من كتاب الأمّ وهذا دليل على أنّ هذا الكتاب كان من مصادر القاضي. راجع: الشافعي، كتاب الأمّ، ج ٧ ص ١١٦–١١٧. راجع أيضا لهذه المسألة: الشافعي، إختلاف الحديث، ص ٥٣٦.

[٨] ناقصة في الأصل واستدركناها من ف.

[٩] الشعر للأعشى، وعجز البيت: كذاك أمور الناس غادٍ وطارقه. ابن قتيبة، أدب الكاتب، ص ٢٩٥.

[١٠] في المخطوطتين: عموما ذكره، ونرجّح أنّ «ذكره» زائدة.

[١١] أبو يعلى، المسند، ج ٨ ص ٣٦٨.

وقوله: الجار أحقّ بِصَقَبه، فالصقب القرب. يقال: هذا أصقب الموضعين أي أقربهما. وقد جاء به بعض أصحاب الحديث بالسين: الجار أحقّ بسقبه،[١٢] ولا أرى في ذلك إلا غلطًا،[١٣] إلا في قول من أجرى السين مجرى الصاد في كلّ شيء. والصقب بإسكان القاف بالصاد والسين، لغتان، وهو الطويل من كلّ شيء،[١٤] وذلك ما لا يدخل في هذا القول. وإنّما هو الصَقَب بفتح القاف والصاد، القرب، يعني أنّ الجار أحقّ بما باعه جاره ممّن ليس بجار. وذلك حقّ القيام بالشفعة في ذلك.[١٥]

والقول [الثابت][١٦] عن أهل البيت صلوات الله عليهم أنّ الشفعة لا تجب
إلا فيما كان من الرباع مشاعًا | غير مقسوم، أو بعضه كذلك، فيبيع أحد ٥٩ ب
الشريكين حصّته منه من غير شريكه فيه. فإن قام الشريك فيه كان أحقّ بالشراء ممّن لا شركة له [فيه][١٧]. فأمّا من ليس له فيه شركة فليس له شفعة وإن كان جارًا لصيقًا أو بعيدًا.

---

[١٢] الشافعي، كتاب الأمّ، ج ٧ ص ١١٦.

[١٣] ولكن راجع: أحمد، المسند، ج ٦ ص ٣٩٠ حيث يورد حديث أبي رافع عن النبي أنه قال: الجار أحق بصقبه أو سقبه.

[١٤] الزبيدي، تاج العروس، مادة س ق ب.

[١٥] يعالج القاضي النعمان مسألة الشفعة في الدعائم. راجع: القاضي النعمان، دعائم الإسلام، ج ٢ ص ٨٧ – ٩٣.

[١٦] ناقصة في الأصل واستدركناها من ف.

[١٧] ناقصة في الأصل واستدركناها من ف.

فإن كان بعض المبيع مشتركًا وبعضه مقسومًا وبيع صفقة واحدة فللشريك في بعضه القيام بالشفعة في كلّ ذلك وأخذه بالثمن [الذي][١٨] بيع به كلّه مقسومه ومشاعه، أو تركه كلّه، وليس له أن يأخذ [من ذلك][١٩] شيئًا دون شيء.

وإن كانت دار بينها وبين دار أخرى حائط، أو ما كان من بنائها ممّا يقع عليه البيع، مشتركًا بين صاحبي الدارين، فالشفعة بذلك [تجب].[٢٠] وإن كان [ذلك][٢١] في حائط عليه حمل الدارين، وهو من حقّ أحدهما دون الآخر، فلا شفعة في ذلك.

٦٠ أ ولا شفعة إلا في العقار وهو الدور والأرض وما هو فيها من الشجر | وغير ذلك ممّا هو مرتبط بها مثل البناء والنبات. فإن كانت الأرض لا تملك ولم يقع البيع عليها، وبيع البناء والنقض، أو النبات والشجر، أو ما هو في الأرض أو عليها دونها، فلا شفعة في ذلك.

وهذا كلّه قول أهل البيت صلوات الله عليهم، ووافقهم عليه جماعة من المنسوبين إلى الفتيا من العوامّ.

---

[١٨] ناقصة في الأصل واستدركناها من ف.

[١٩] ناقصة في الأصل واستدركناها من ف.

[٢٠] ناقصة في الأصل واستدركناها من ف.

[٢١] ناقصة في الأصل واستدركناها من ف.

وخالفهم آخرون فيما سوى ذلك وأوجبوا للجار الملاصق الشفعة دون البعيد، واحتجّوا بهذا الحديث ورووه عن رسول الله صلى الله عليه وعلى آله أنه قال: الجار أحقّ بصقبه.

وعلل آخرون هذا الحديث وذكروا اختلاف الروّاة فيه واضطراب قولهم. قالوا: فدلّ ذلك على أنّ الحديث غير محفوظ، ورووا عن[٢٢] رسول الله صلى الله عليه وعلى آله أنّه قال: الشفعة في كلّ شرك في أرض أو ربع أو
٦٠ ب حائط، لا يصلح أن يبيع حتى يعرض على شريكه فيأخذ أو يدع. فإن أبى فشريكه أحقّ به حتى يؤذنه،[٢٣] وأنّ رسول الله صلى الله عليه وعلى آله قضى بالشفعة فيما لم يقسم، فإذا وقعت الحدود فلا شفعة.[٢٤] وهذا قول أكثر العامّة.

وقال بعضهم: إن ثبت الحديث الجار أحقّ بصقبه، فالمراد بالجار هاهنا الشريك، لأنّ الحديث الذي جاء بأنّ الشفعة للشريك، [فإذا وقعت الحدود][٢٥] فلا شفعة، يقضي عليه ويبيّنه. وقد يكون ذلك مجملا وهذا

---

[٢٢] الأصل: أن، وأثبتنا النصّ من ف وهو الصحيح.
[٢٣] أورده مسلم بلفظه. راجع مسلم، الصحيح، ج ٥ ص ٥٧.
[٢٤] مالك بن أنس، الموطأ، ج ٢ ص ٧١٤.
[٢٥] ناقصة في الأصل واستدركناها من ف.

مفسّرًا، والمفسّر يقضي على المجمل، ولأنّ الذين أوجبوا الشفعة بالجوار، وقد قالوا الشريك أحقّ بها من الجار الملاصق، ولم يوجبوا لغير الملاصق شفعة، وإن كان اسم الجار يقع عليه ولا لغيره ممّن ذكرت أنّ اسم الجوار يلزمه. فلو سلم لهم هذا الحديث: الجار أحقّ بصقبه، وأثبت ولم تكن فيه علة، لوجب أن يقضى بالشفعة لجميع الجيران ولم يجب أن يخصّوا بها الملاصق منهم | دون غيره. ٦١ أ

وعامّتهم يقولون: من أوصى لجيرانه أعطى الملاصق منهم وغير الملاصق.

وقال آخرون ممّن دفع شفعة غير الشريك: لو صحّ الحديث الجار أحقّ بصقبه، لم يكن ممّا يعارض الحديث الذي فيه الشفعة للشريك.

ولا شفعة فيما وقعت عليه الحدود، لأنّ قوله: الجار أحقّ بصقبه، ليس فيه ذكر الشفعة. قد يكون الجار أحقّ بما قرب منه ممّن بعد عنه، كالرحبة والطريق الواسع والمباح يكون بجوار دار الرجل فهو أحقّ بالانتفاع به ممّن بعد عنه ولم يجاوره وما أشبه ذلك ممّا يكون القريب أولى به من البعيد عنه.

وقوله: الجار أحقّ بصقبه، إذا ثبت وكان المراد الشفعة للشريك كما تقدّم القول بأنه يقع عليه اسم الجار ولأنّه أقرب من الجار الملاصق لأنّه مخالط من جميع الجهات، قول مجمل. وإنّما يكون ذلك كما ذكرنا في | الرباع خاصّة ٦١ ب
دون سائر الأشياء، فلو حُمِلَ على ظاهره لكان في جميعها.

ومن ذلك أيضًا أنّ الشريك [إنّما يكون][٢٦] أحقّ بالشفعة في حين البيع وبعد أن ينعقد وفيما بينه وبين أن تمضي سنة. فإن مضت ولم يقم بالشفعة فلا شفعة له. هذا قول أهل البيت صلوات الله عليهم ووافقهم عليه بعض العامّة.

وقال آخرون من العامّة: إذا علم الشفيع بالبيع فلم يقم فيه في الوقت انقطعت شفعته.

وقال آخرون: إن أخّر القيام لعُذرٍ فله أن يطلب بها وعليه اليمين أنّه ما تركها رضىً منه بالتسليم.

وقال آخرون: إذا كان حاضرًا للبيع فلم يقم فلا شفعة له.

وقال آخرون: له القيام بالشفعة بعد علمه بالبيع بثلاثة أيّام فما دونها، فإذا مضت عليه ثلاثة أيّام بعد أن علم فلا شفعة له.

[وقال آخرون: إذا مضى يوم فلا شفعة له].[٢٧]

وقال آخرون: له الشفعة، متى قام فيها أخذها.

وإذا قام الشفيع | على المشتري بالشفعة فأخذها من يده ودفع إليه ما اشترى ٦٢ أ
[به][٢٨]، ثمّ استحقّ ذلك عليه وأخرج بالحكم من يديه، رجع بالثمن على

[٢٦] ناقصة في الأصل واستدركناها من ف.

[٢٧] ناقصة في الأصل واستدركناها من ف.

[٢٨] ناقصة في الأصل واستدركناها من ف.

البائع الذي كان قبضه من المشتري الأوّل[٢٩] في قول أهل البيت صلوات الله عليهم، ووافقهم على ذلك فريق من العامّة.

وخالفهم آخرون فقالوا: يرجع بذلك على المشتري الذي دفعه إليه ويرجع به المشتري على البائع.

والشفعة للغائب حتى يحضر وللصغير حتى يكبر. فإذا قدم الغائب فله القيام بالشفعة ما بينه وبين الوقت الذي بلغه البيع فيه حيث[٣٠] كان وبين مدّة سنة. فإن بلغه ذلك وهو غائب ولم يقم بالشفعة حتى مضت السنة لم تكن له شفعة. وإن قام فيها فيما بينه وبين السنة فله القيام بذلك.[٣١]

والطفل يقوم إذا بلغ[٣٢] بشفعته في حين بلوغه، وإن مضى للبيع أكثر من السنة،
إلا أن يكون له وصيّ | أو وليّ يجوز أمره عليه فيسلمها. وإن قام الوصيّ له ٦٢ ب
بها كان له القيام.

---

[٢٩] القاضي النعمان، دعائم الإسلام، ج ٢ ص ٨٧، حيث أورد المحقق فيضي في حواشي تحقيقه هذا النص من ذات البيان من قوله: وإذا قام الشفيع إلخ...

[٣٠] الأصل: حين، وأثبتنا النصّ من ف وهو أصحّ.

[٣١] ذكر القاضي النعمان هذه الفقرة في كتاب الاقتصار على النحو التالي: والشفعة للصغير حتى يكبر وللغائب حتى يحضر وللحاضر البالغ ما بينه وبين سنة إلا أن يسلم البيع. راجع: القاضي النعمان، الاقتصار، ص ٩٣.

[٣٢] كتبت في الهامش بنفس الخط.

وهذا قول أهل البيت صلوات الله عليهم ووافقهم عليه [فريق][٣٣] من العامّة.

وقال بعضهم: لا شفعة للغائب ولا للطفل.

والشفعة لليهود والنصارى فيما بينهم بعضهم على بعض كما هي للمسلمين فيما[٣٤] بينهم. ولا شفعة لهم على المسلمين في قول أهل البيت صلوات الله عليهم، ووافقهم على ذلك فريق من العامّة.

وقال آخرون منهم: الشفعة لهم على المسلمين كما هي عليهم.

ولا شفعة في حيوان في قول أهل البيت صلوات الله عليهم، ووافقهم على ذلك سائر أهل الفتيا من العامّة.

وإن كان عبد بين رجلين فباع أحدهما نصيبه منه، فإنّ شريكه فيه أحقّ بذلك في قول أهل البيت صلوات الله عليهم.

وما اشتُرِيَ من المشاع من الرباع بعروض لها مثل معلوم، فقام الشريك فيه، فله
٦٣ أ القيام بذلك | ويدفع مثل ذلك من العروض.

وما لم يكن له مثل معلوم فلا شفعة فيما يبيع به. وما دُفِعَ[٣٥] في صداق امرأة من ذلك أو وُهِبَ أو تُصُدِّق به، فلا شفعة فيه إلا أن يكون عقد الصداق

[٣٣] ناقصة في الأصل واستدركناها من هامش ف.
[٣٤] كتبت في هامش الأصل بنفس الخط.
[٣٥] الأصل: ولا دفع، وأثبتنا النصّ من ف وهو أصحّ.

على عين ودفع في ذلك [بعد][٣٦] العقد على العين مشاع من الرباع، فذلك مثل البيع وللشريك فيه القيام بالشفعة.

وإذا اشترى المشتري ما تجب فيه الشفعة فبنى فيه وأصلح وعمّر وأنفق على ذلك، ثمّ قام عليه الشفيع فعليه أن يدفع إليه ما اشتراه به وما أنفقه، إن شاء أخذ بذلك وإن شاء تركه له ما اشتراه وسلمه.

وإن اشترى المشتري ما تجب فيه الشفعة بنسيئة إلى أجل، فقام عليه الشفيع، فإن كان ثقة مليًّا بالثمن فهو عليه إلى وقت الأجل الذي بيع إليه. وإن لم يكن مليًّا بذلك أو غير ثقة به وأعطى بذلك كفيلا ثقة مليًّا فله ذلك. وإن لم يجد ذلك، فإن شاء أن يعجّل الثمن أو يسلم الشفعة، وليس عليه | ٦٣ ب غير ذلك.

وما اشتُرِيَ من الدور التي لا يملك أرضها البائع وإنّما بيع نقضها، فليس في ذلك شفعة.

وإذا كانت دار ذات علوّ وسفل بين الرجلين واقتسماها، فصار العلوّ لأحدهما والسفل للآخر، أو بعض هذا وبعض هذا لكلّ واحد، فباع أحدهما، فليس في ذلك شفعة إذا كان مقسومًا معلومًا، إلا أن يكون بقي

---

[٣٦] ناقصة في الأصل واستدركاها من ف.

بينهما في ذلك شيء مشاع، مثل حائط بينهما أو مدخل أو مطلع أو ما أشبه ذلك. فإن كان ذلك وجبت به الشفعة.

وإذا كانت دار ذات مساكن أو رائعة غير نافذة ومدخل أهل الدار إليها مشترك بينهم، ليس كالطريق السابل، فبيع من هذه الدور شيء فالشركاء[٣٧] في المدخل شفعاء فيما بيع من ذلك، ومن قام منهم فله القيام.

وإذا باع واحد بعد واحد ما فيه الشفعة فللشفيع أن يقوم على أيّهم شاء منهم.

٦٤ أ وإذا قام الشفيع بالشفعة فقد لزمه | أن يدفع الثمن إلى المشتري إن كان دفعه، أو إلى البائع إن كان لم يقبضه. فإن قام بها ثمّ ترك القيام، وأراد المشتري أن يقوم عليه بدفع ما اشتراه إليه وأخذ ثمنه، فله ذلك إن كان قد قام عليه به.

وإن كان المبيع فيه شركاء جماعة فقام أحدهم ولم يقم الآخرون، فله أن يأخذ جميع ما وقع البيع. وإن قاموا كلّهم أو بعضهم فلمن قام منهم أن يأخذ بها دون من لم يقم، ويصير ذلك بينهم[٣٨] دون من لم يقم منهم.

---

[٣٧] الأصل: كالشركاء، وأثبتنا النصّ من ف وهو أصحّ.

[٣٨] القاضي النعمان، دعائم الإسلام، ج ٢ ص ٨٧، حيث أورد المحقق فيضي في حواشي تحقيقه هذا النص من ذات البيان من قوله: وإن كان المبيع، إلخ...

وهذا كلّه قول أهل البيت صلوات الله عليهم ووافقهم المنسوبون إلى الفتيا من العامّة في كثير منه وخالفوهم في بعضه.

والوقوف على هذا ومثله هو الذي يغني منه من أراد علمه، لا ما زعم ابن قتيبة أنّه يغني من ذلك معرفة قوله:[٣٩] الجار أحقّ بصقبه. بل يكون معرفة من عرف ذلك ولم يعلم ما حقيقة الجار، وما الصقب، وما قيل ذلك فيه، وأنّ القول بذلك | وكثير ممّا ذكره مجمل محتاج إلى البيان. وإذا لم يعلم من ٦٤ ب
بيان ذلك بتطويل الفقهاء، ما زعم ابن قتيبة أنه يُستغنى عنه، فما استغنى إلا بالجهل عن العلم الذي [استغنى][٤٠] هو بمثله.

وهذه[٤١] جمل من القول في البيان في هذا الباب ذكرتها مختصرة وتتفرّع منها فروع كثيرة ومسائل عديدة. ولكنّ من علم هذه الأصول دعاه العلم بها، إذا وُفِّق لمحبّة العلم واختار أن يبين به من صفة الجهّال، إلى البحث عن ذلك والتبحّر فيه. فإنّ العلم ما زيد المرء منه ازداد به رفعة.[٤٢] قال الله جلّ من

---

[٣٩] الأصل: قوله معرفة، وأثبتنا النصّ من ف وهو أصحّ.

[٤٠] ناقصة في الأصل واستدركناها من ف.

[٤١] الأصل: وهذا، وأثبتنا النصّ من ف وهو أصحّ.

[٤٢] الأصل مضطرب وبيانه: فان العلم ما زيد المرء اذا زاد به رفعة، وأثبتنا النصّ من ف وهو أوضح.

قائل: ﴿يَرْفَعِ اللَّهُ الَّذِينَ آمَنُوا مِنكُمْ وَالَّذِينَ أُوتُوا الْعِلْمَ دَرَجَاتٍ﴾.[٤٣] والله يهدي من أحبّ بفضل نعمته.

تمّ الجزء السادس من ذات البيان

والحمد لله ربّ العالمين.

يتلوه في الجزء السابع

ذكر بيان قوله: والطلاق بالرجال والعدّة بالنساء.

[٤٣] المجادلة ٥٨/١١.

| الجزء السابع من ذات البيان ٦٥ أ

من تأليف القاضي النعمان بن محمد

قدّس الله روحه ورزقنا شفاعته وأنسه

بحقّ محمد وآله الطيّبين الطاهرين

صلوات الله عليهم أجمعين

| بسم الله الرحمن الرحيم ٦٥ ب

ذكر بيان قوله:

الطلاق بالرجال والعدّة بالنساء

هذا قول حكاه ابن قتيبة عن رسول الله صلى اله عليه وعلى آله على ما رسمه في أوّل قوله الذي حكيناه عنه. ولا أعلم أحدًا رواه عن رسول الله صلى الله عليه وعلى آله،[1] وإنّما روى ذلك بعض العامّة عن بعض الصحابة. وسنذكر من روى ذلك عنه ومن قال به.

---

[1] بل قد يروى مرفوعا عن الرسول، ولو أنه في الغالب يروى موقوفا على الصحابة، راجع: الدارقطني، العلل، ج ٥ ص ١٩٥.

ومعنى ذلك وبيانه أن تكون الحرّة تحت المملوك فيطلقها ولا يبينها منه حتى تحرم إلا ثلاث تطليقات، كما قال الله جلّ ذكره: ﴿الطَّلَاقُ مَرَّتَانِ فَإِمْسَاكٌ بِمَعْرُوفٍ أَوْ تَسْرِيحٌ بِإِحْسَانٍ﴾،[٢] يعني أن يطلقها ثالثة إن لم يرد أن يمسكها فتبين منه بثلاث تطليقات.

وهذا [هو][٣] قول أهل البيت صلوات الله عليهم [إنّه][٤] إذا كانت المرأة حرّة، عند حرّ كانت أو عند مملوك، فلا يزيل عصمته عنها ويحلها لغيره[٥] وتحرم
٦٦ أ عليه حتى تنكح زوجًا غيره إذا طلقها للعدّة إلا ثلاث تطليقات. | وعليها أن تعتدّ بثلاثة قروء إن كانت ممّن تحيض وكان قد دخل بها، أو بثلاثة أشهر أن لم تكن تحيض.

فإن كانت أمة عند حرّ أو عند مملوك فطلقها تطليقتين للعدّة بانت منه وحلت للأزواج غيره. وتعتدّ بحيضتين إن كان[٦] قد دخل بها وكانت تحيض لأنّ عليها من العدّة نصف ما على الحرّة. كذلك الطلاق، لأنّ الطلاق والحيض

---

[٢] البقرة ٢/٢٢٩.
[٣] ناقصة في الأصل واستدركناها من ف.
[٤] ناقصة في الأصل واستدركناها من ف.
[٥] الأصل شديد الاضطراب وبيانه: فلا يزيل عصمة عنها ويحرم لغيره، وأثبتنا النصّ من ف وهو الصواب.
[٦] الأصل: كانت، وأثبتنا النصّ من ف وهو أصحّ.

لا يتجزّآن، فصار طلاقها تطليقتين وعدّتها حيضتين. فإن لم تكن تحيض اعتدّت بشهر ونصف.

هذا قول أهل البيت عليهم السلام، وقالوا: الطلاق والعدّة بالنساء لأنّ ذلك من أحكامهنّ. قال الله جلّ من قائل: ﴿يَا أَيُّهَا النَّبِيُّ إِذَا طَلَّقْتُمُ النِّسَاء فَطَلِّقُوهُنَّ لِعِدَّتِهِنَّ﴾.[٧] فبقدر ما يلزمهنّ من العدّة كذلك يلزمهنّ [من الطلاق][٨] على ظاهر قول الله عزّ وجلّ هذا الذي تلوناه.

وواقف أهل البيت صلوات الله عليهم في أنّ عدّة الأمة التي | تحيض حيضتين ٦٦ ب
كافّة أهل الفتيا من العوامّ ولا أعلم أحدًا قال بخلاف ذلك غير الشعبي وابن سيرين، فإنهما قالا: عدّتها كعدّة الحرّة ثلاث حيض.[٩]

واختلفوا فيها إذا كانت لا تحيض، صغيرة لم تبلغ المحيض أو كبيرة قد يئست منه، فوافق فريق منهم قول أهل البيت صلوات الله عليهم أنّ عدّتها شهر ونصف.

وقال آخرون: تعتدّ شهرين.

وقال آخرون: تعتدّ ثلاثة أشهر كما تعتدّ الحرّة.

---

[٧] الطلاق ٦٥/١.

[٨] ناقصة في الأصل واستدركاها من ف.

[٩] نقل ابن عبد البر رأي ابن سيرين هذا ويبدو أنه رأي أهل الظاهر. راجع: ابن كثير، تفسير القرآن، ج ١ ص ٢٧٠.

وأجمعوا على أنّ عدّة الأمة في الوفاة نصف عدّة الحرّة إذا لم تكن حاملا، فرجعوا إلى قول أهل البيت صلوات الله عليهم في المملوكة المتوفى عنها زوجها.

وخالفهم بعضهم في المطلقة كما ذكرنا فقالوا: تعتدّ شهرين وخمسة أيّام ما خلا ابن سيرين فإنّه قال: عليها مثل عدّة الحرّة أربعة أشهر وعشر.

٦٧ أ وقال من قال من العامّة: الطلاق بالرجل والعدّة بالنساء، كالقول الذي | حكاه ابن قتيبة في أوّل هذا الباب ونسبه إلى رسول الله صلى الله عليه وعلى آله، ولم أعلم أحدًا غيره نسبه إليه. وأكثر ما جاء ذلك ورواه من قال بهذا القول أنّ غلامًا لعائشة كانت تحته امرأة حرّة، فطلقها تطليقتين ثمّ أراد أن يراجعها، فأتى عائشة فسألها، فقالت له لا تقربها حتى تسأل[1] عن ذلك. فسأل عنه عثمان بن عفّان فقال له: لا تقربها. فانصرف إلى عائشة فأخبرها، فقالت له: سل زيد بن ثابت، فسأله فقال: لا تقربها.[2]

---

[1] الأصل: حتى تسأله، وأثبتنا النصّ من ف وهو أصحّ.

[2] الرواية المشهورة لهذه الحادثة أنّ نفيعا، وهو مكاتب أو عبد لأمّ سلمة زوج النبّي، كانت تحته امرأة حرّة فطلقها اثنتين وأراد أن يراجعها. فأمره أزواج النبيّ أن يسأل عثمان بن عفان، فلقي عثمان، ومعه زيد بن ثابت فقالا له: حرمت عليك. راجع: مالك بن أنس، الموطأ، ج ٢ ص ٥٧٤. ولم نعثر على هذه الحادثة مقرونة بعائشة كما يرويها القاضي النعمان هنا.

ورووا عنه وعن ابن عبّاس أنهما قالا: الطلاق بالرجال والعدّة بالنساء، ومعنى ذلك أنّ المملوك إذا كانت عنده حرّة أو أمة فطلقها تطليقتين بانت منه، لأنّ طلاقه نصف طلاق الحرّ. والطلاق لا يتجزّأ، وإن كان حرًّا عنده أمة أو حرّة لم يَبِنْها منه في قول من يقول | بهذا القول إلا ثلاث ٦٧ ب
تطليقات.

فهذا معنى قولهم: الطلاق بالرجال، أي [يجري][١٢] على حكمهم، إن كانوا أحرارًا طلقوا ثلاثًا وإن كانوا مماليكَ طلقوا تطليقتين من كانت عندهم من حرّة أو أمة.

ومعنى قولهم: العدّة بالنساء، أنّ الحرّة تعتدّ ثلاث حيض، إن كانت تحيض، من الطلاق. فإن لم تكن تحيض اعتدّت ثلاثة أشهر من طلاق مَن طلقها من زوج، مَن كان من حرّ أو عبد. وتعتدّ الأمة من الطلاق، إن كانت تحيض، عدّة الأمة.

وقد ذكرت قولهم في ذلك عند من كانت من حرّ وعبد بقول أهل البيت صلوات الله عليهم: الطلاق والعدّة بالنساء،[١٣] طلاق الحرّ والعبد الحرّة ثلاث تطليقات، فإن كانت تحيض فأجلها ثلاثة قروء وإن كانت لا تحيض فأجلها

---

[١٢] ناقصة في الأصل واستدركناها من ف.

[١٣] راجع: القاضي النعمان، دعائم الإسلام، ج ٢ ص ٣٠؛ الشيخ الصدوق، الفقيه، ج ٣ ص ٥٤٢؛ أبو عبيد، غريب الحديث، ج ٣ ص ٤٣٤.

ثلاثة أشهر. وطلاق الحرّ والعبد الأمة تطليقتين، فإن كانت تحيض فأجلها حيضتان وإن تكن لا تحيض فأجلها شهر ونصف. وعدّة الحرّة في الوفاة من
٦٨ أ الحرّ | والمملوك أربعة أشهر وعشر، وعدّة المملوكة من الحرّ ومن المملوك شهران وخمس ليال. والحامل المطلقة أجلها أن تضع حملها، حرّة كانت أم مملوكة. والمتوفى عنها زوجها الحامل تعتدّ أبعد الأجلين: إن وضعت قبل تمام العدّة تربّصت حتى تبلغ العدّة، وإن بلغت العدّة ولم تضع تربّصت حتى تضع.

ووافق أهل البيت صلوات الله عليهم في أنّ أجل الحامل المطلقة أن تضع حملها جميع أهل الفتيا من العامّة، حرّة كانت أو مملوكة أو ما كانت. ووافقهم بعضهم في أنّ الحامل المتوفى عنها زوجها أجلها آخر الأجلين. وفارقهم آخرون فقالوا: أجلها أن تضع ما في بطنها، فإذا وضعته فقد انقضت عدّتها متى وضعته.

وقد ذكرت في غير موضع من هذا الكتاب وغيره أنّ قول أهل البيت صلوات
٦٨ ب الله عليهم هو قول رسول الله صلى | الله عليه وعلى آله لأنهم عنه أخذوه، ومن خالفهم فإنّما قال برأيه مع ما ذكرت في هذا الباب ممّا يثبت قولهم ويشدّه من ظاهر قول الله عزّ وجلّ: ﴿يَا أَيُّهَا النَّبِيُّ إِذَا طَلَّقْتُمُ النِّسَاء فَطَلِّقُوهُنَّ

لِعِدَّتِهِنَّ ﴾ .[١٤] فأوجب عزّ وجلّ الطلاق للعدّة، وهو ما بيّن أنّ الطلاق والعدّة بالنساء كما قال أهل البيت صلوات الله عليهم وآثروا ذلك عن رسول الله صلى الله عليه وعلى آله، لا على قول ابن قتيبة ومن قال مثل قوله إنّ الطلاق بالرجال والعدّة بالنساء، فيكون الحرّ يطلق الأمة ثلاثًا طلاقًا كاملا وتعتدّ نصف عدّة الحرّة،[١٥] أو يطلق المملوك الحرّة تطليقتين وتعتدّ ثلاث حيض، أو[١٦] ثلاثة أشهر إن كانت لا تحيض، كما قال بذلك من قال به من العامّة. وهذا خلاف الطلاق الذي أمر الله عزّ وجلّ به للعدّة. وإنّما يقع كلّ تطليقة على حيضة، فإذا لم تكن كذلك لم يكن الطلاق للعدّة.

٦٩ أ | وأكثر ما احتجّ به في ذلك من قال بذلك من العامّة، أعني قولهم: الطلاق بالرجال والعدّة بالنساء، أنّ الله عزّ وجلّ خاطب بالطلاق الرجال وبالعدّة النساء، فقال: ﴿يَا أَيُّهَا النَّبِيُّ إِذَا طَلَّقْتُمُ النِّسَاء فَطَلِّقُوهُنَّ لِعِدَّتِهِنَّ﴾،[١٧] وقال: ﴿وَإِذَا طَلَّقْتُمُ النَّسَاءَ فَبَلَغْنَ أَجَلَهُنَّ﴾،[١٨] وقال في العدّة: ﴿وَالَّذِينَ

---

[١٤] الطلاق ٦٥/١.

[١٥] الأصل: الحر، وأثبتنا النصّ من ف وهو الصواب.

[١٦] الأصل: وثلاثة، وأثبتنا النصّ من ف وهو الصواب.

[١٧] الطلاق ٦٥/١.

[١٨] البقرة ٢/٢٣١–٢٣٢.

يُتَوَفَّوْنَ مِنكُمْ وَيَذَرُونَ أَزْوَاجًا يَتَرَبَّصْنَ بِأَنفُسِهِنَّ أَرْبَعَةَ أَشْهُرٍ وَعَشْرًا ﴾،[١٩]
وقال: ﴿ وَالْمُطَلَّقَاتُ يَتَرَبَّصْنَ بِأَنفُسِهِنَّ ثَلاثَةَ قُرُوءٍ ﴾.[٢٠]

ولا أدري أيّ حجّة لهذا القائل ومن قال بقوله في المخاطبة، والحكم من الله عزّ وجلّ يجري مجرًى واحدًا[٢١] بإجماع لمن عناه بالخطاب، خاطبه بذلك أم لم يخاطبه. وقد خاطب بالقرآن الذين كانوا في عصر الرسول عليه السلام وجرى حكمه على من بعدهم ممّن لم يخاطبه بمثل ما خاطب أولائك ممّا تعبّد العباد [به].[٢٢] وهذا إجماع لا اختلاف فيه ولكنّ هذه
٦٩ ب استراحات | أهل الباطل. فيدع هذا القائل من قول الله عزّ وجلّ ذكره ما فيه البيان، وذلك قوله الذي تلوناه: ﴿يَا أَيُّهَا النَّبِيُّ إِذَا طَلَّقْتُمُ النِّسَاء فَطَلِّقُوهُنَّ لِعِدَّتِهِنَّ﴾،[٢٣] ويحتجّ بالخطاب ويتأوّل من ذات نفسه تأويلا يشهد القرآن ببطلانه كما ذكرناه.

---

[١٩] البقرة ٢/٢٣٤.
[٢٠] البقرة ٢/٢٢٨.
[٢١] الأصل: مجرى واحد، وأثبتنا النصّ من ف وهو الصواب.
[٢٢] ناقصة في الأصل واستدركناها من ف.
[٢٣] الطلاق ٦٥/١.

وجميع الأمّة على القول في الخطاب على ما وصفنا . ولولا ذلك لم تلزم الفرائض إلا الذين خوطبوا بها في وقت نزولها وسقطت عمّن بعدهم ممّن لا يُخاطَب بها .

ثمّ قال هذا القائل: قد أجمعوا أنّ الحرّ إذا كانت عنده حرّة لم يحرمها عليه حتى تنكح زوجًا غيره إلا ثلاث تطليقات.

واختلفوا في الحرّ يكون تحته الأمة فيطلقها تطليقتين. فقالت طائفة: قد حرمت عليه حتى تنكح زوجًا غيره. وقال آخرون: له أن يراجعها وغير جائز أن تحرم عليه رجعتها إلا بحجّة من كتاب أو سنة أو إجماع.

قال: فلا سبيل | لمن خالَفَنا إثبات ذلك. فقطع هذا القائل على خصمه ٧٠ أ
وحتّم[٢٤] عليه أنّه لا سبيل له إلى ما ذكره.

فأمّا الحجّة من الكتاب فقد ذكرناها من قول الله عزّ وجلّ: ﴿يَا أَيُّهَا النَّبِيُّ إِذَا طَلَّقْتُمُ النِّسَاء فَطَلِّقُوهُنَّ لِعِدَّتِهِنَّ﴾،[٢٥] وبيّنّا ذلك.

وأمّا السنّة فقد أوضحنا أنّ ما جاء عن أئمّتنا فهو منقول إليهم بواحد عن واحد منهم عن رسول الله صلى الله عليه وعلى آله، بذلك أخبرَنا أوّلهم عن آخرهم، ورووه كذلك لنا ، وأخبرونا أنّهم لم يقولوا شيئًا برأيهم، وحذّرونا من

---

[٢٤] الأصل: ختم، وأثبتنا النصّ من ف وهو الصواب.

[٢٥] الطلاق ٦٥/١.

القول بالرأي في دين الله سبحانه، وأعابوا بذلك من قاله، ونهوا عن متابعته على قوله وعلى من لم يعلم بذلك عن الرسول عليه السلام ممّن علمه ورواه عنه صلى الله عليه وعلى آله.

وأمّا الإجماع فقد أجمعوا كما حكيناه عنهم أنّ عدّة الأمة في الوفاة نصف عدّة الحرّة. فقد أوجدنا هذا القائل الثلاثة | التي حكم علينا بأنّا لا نجد ٧٠ ب
وجهًا منه وأنه لا سبيل لنا إليه. إنّ سبيلنا إلى ذلك وإلى غيره من الحقّ سبيل الله عزّ وجلّ التي تنكّبها هو وأمثاله وتاهوا في سبيل الضلالات بتنكّبهم عنها. ولو قصدوها لردّتهم إلى رضوان الله ربّهم وعصمتهم من القول في دينه بأهوائهم وآرائهم.

وأمّا قوله: غير جائز أن تحرم رجعتها إلا بحجّة، فقد أوجدنا من قال بقوله إيّاها وبعكس قول صاحبه عليه، فنقول له: غير جائز أن تحلّ له رجعتها إلا بحجة من كتاب أو سنّة أو إجماع. ولا سبيل له هو إلى ذلك إلا سبيل الباطل التي جمح فيها. وقياسه، وإن كان القياس فاسدًا من أصله، الحرّة بالمملوكة وحكمها في العدّة مختلف، قياس فاسد عند من قال بالقياس من أمثاله.

وهذا قول محمد بن إبراهيم بن المنذر[٢٦] [واحتجاجه]،[٢٧] وهو عند العامّة من رؤساء المتعقّبين والنُظّار بزعمهم. والناظر من | نظر بنور الله واتّبع ما جاء ٧١ أ
عنه بالأخذ من أوليائه الذين أمر الله عزّ وجلّ باتّباعهم والأخذ عنهم وردّ ما اختلِف فيه إليهم، لا من نظر بهواه واجتباه وردّ ما اختُلِف فيه إلى قياسه ورأيه واستحسانه. وقد نهى الله عزّ وجلّ عن ذلك في كتابه وعلى لسان رسوله صلى الله عليه وعلى آله وأمر باتّباع ما أنزله وردّ من لم يعلم إلى أهل الذكر أوليائه ما جهله.

فهذا بيان ما ذكره ابن قتيبة من قوله: الطلاق بالرجل والعدّة بالنساء، وأوهم أنّه عن رسول الله صلى الله عليه وعلى آله، وليس هو عنه. ولو جاء عنه صلى الله عليه وعلى آله لاحتجّ به من قال به من العامّة، ولو كان لا يثبت، كما احتجّوا بغير ذلك من مثل ما نسبوه إلى رسول الله صلى الله عليه وعلى آله ولم يثبت عنه. وبمثل هذا من التدليس والتورية والتشبيه بالباطل على
[أهل][٢٨] الحقّ يكذبون على الله وعلى | رسوله. ٧١ ب

[٢٦] محمد بن إبراهيم بن المنذر النيسابوري، أبو بكر، المتوفى ٣١٨ هـ. راجع عنه: الذهبي، سير، ج ١٤ ص ٤٩٠–٤٩٢.

[٢٧] ناقصة في الأصل واستدركناها من ف.

[٢٨] ناقصة في الأصل واستدركناها من ف.

ولولا البيان وما رغب عنه ابن قتيبة من يعلم هذا ومثله عن إطالة الفقهاء بزعمه، ليجوز عنده من باطله مثل هذا وغيره، إذا سلم لقوله وأخذ به واقتصر عليه ورغب عن البيان الذي رغب به عنه وأوهمه أنّ ما ألقاه إليه يغنيه عنه، لم يكن يحظى إلا بالكذب [الذي][29] كذبه له على رسول الله صلى الله عليه وعلى آله. وقد قال عليه السلام: من كذب عليّ متعمّدا فليتبوّأ مقعده من النار، سيّما في إباحة ما حظّره الله عزّ وجلّ وتحليل ما حرّمه من الفروج التي ارتكابها بغير حلها من الكبائر التي تواعد الله عزّ وجلّ بالنار عليها.

ثمّ لم يكن يعلم من ذلك لو اقتصر على قوله دون إطالة الفقهاء التي [أعابها][30] عنده إلا ما هو بجهله أعذر منه بعلمه، وذلك إن لم يكن يعلم إلا قوله: الطلاق بالرجال والعدّة بالنساء، وهو لا يدري ما معنى ذلك ولا ما الجواب
٧٢ أ فيه إذا | سئل عنه، ولا باطله من حقّه وصوابه من خطئه. فما أراد به إلا أن يغرقه في الجهل الذي هو فيه من دينه.

ولم يقتصر به كذلك في هذا الكتاب الذي حكى هذا القول فيه في غير علم الدين، بل تعمّق به في كثير من العلوم الدنياويّة تعمقًا جاوز حدود الكفاية

---

[29] ناقصة في الأصل واستدركناها من ف.

[30] ناقصة في الأصل واستدركناها من ف.

لمن بسط له مثل ذلك على ما رتّبه عليه وعمد إلى ما يلزمه علمه ومعرفته، وهو مفروض عليه، فحذفه له عن آخره و[اقتصر به منه على ما هو يجهله لو بقي فيه، أعذر منه بعلمه ما][٣١] اقتصر به عليه، رغبة عن العلم واطراحًا له وزهادة فيه.

والله يهدي ويوفق لعلمه من يرتضيه[٣٢] وإن صدّ عنه هذا الصادّ عن دين الله وأمثاله وحرّفوا الكلم فيه عن مواضعه.

تمّ الجزء السابع من ذات البيان والحمد لله ربّ العلمين.

يتلوه في الجزء الثامن

ذكر بيان النهي عن المخابرة

---

[٣١] ناقصة في الأصل واستدركناها من ف.

[٣٢] الأصل: من بريته، وأثبتنا النصّ من ف وهو أصحّ.

٧٢ ب | الجزء الثامن من ذات البيان

من تأليف القاضي النعمان بن محمد

قدّس الله روحه ورزقنا شفاعته وأنسه

بحقّ محمد وآله الطيّبين الطاهرين

صلوات الله عليهم أجمعين.

٧٣ أ

| ذكر بيان
النهي عن المخابرة

المخابرة والخبر المزارعة على النصف أو الثلث أو الربع،[١] أو ما اشترط من ذلك ممّا تخرج الأرض من ذلك يكون لربّ الأرض يأخذه ممّن يزرعها ويحرثها ببذره ودوابه ونفسه.

والمخابرة في اللغة المؤاكرة، وذلك عمل الأُكّار[٢] وهم المزارعون على ما ذكرته في الأرض، وهم العاملون. والمخابرة بمعنى المعاملة. وقيل إنّ ذلك إنّما اشتقّ لها من خيبر لأنّ أهلها عملوا فيها كذلك.[٣]

---

[١] راجع: أبو عبيد، غريب الحديث، ج ١ ص ٢٣٢.

[٢] كذا في المخطوطتين، كأنّها جمع الأَكّار وهو المزارع. إلا أنّنا لم نجد هذا الجمع في المعاجم، فإنّ جمع الأكّار الأَكَرة. راجع: ابن منظور، لسان العرب، مادّة أ ك ر.

[٣] راجع: ابن قتيبة، غريب الحديث، ج ١ ص ٣٠.

وهذا اللفظ، أعني المخابرة، من لفظ الرواة ولم يؤثروه كذلك من لفظ النبيّ صلى الله عليه وعلى آله. وقد روي من طريق العامّة أنّ رسول الله صلى الله عليه وعلى آله نهى عن المخابرة،[٤] فتمسّك بعضهم بهذا الخبر ولم يروا المزارعة بالنصف والثلث ونحو ذلك ممّا تخرج الأرض.

فأمّا أهل البيت صلوات الله عليهم فإنّهم يجيزون ذلك ولا يرون به بأسًا. | ٧٣ ب
وكذلك قالوا: أعطى رسول الله صلى الله عليه وعلى آله خيبر على الشطر ممّا تخرج وفيها نخل وشجر وأرض كانت ممّا أفاء الله عليه، فأخذها منه أهلها من اليهود على ذلك. فلمّا كان أوان جداد النخل بعث إليهم عبد الله بن رواحة الأنصاري ليخرص ذلك عليهم، فخرصه، فقالوا: كيف تلزمنا شيئًا إنّما تظنّه ظنًّا بلا حقيقة؟ فقال لهم: أنتم بخير النظيرَيْن: إن شئتم فخذوه بما خرصته وأعطونا نصف ذلك، وإن شئتم فسلموه لنا وخذوا نصف ما خرصناه به. فقالت اليهود: بهذا قامت السموات والأرض.[٥]

وهذا حديث [معروف][٦] مشهور ولكنّ الذين أنكروا وأبطلوا المزارعة بالربع والثلث والنصف وأشباه ذلك زعموا أنّ ذلك يجوز في مساقاة النخل والشجر

---

[٤] ابن أبي شيبة، المصنف، ج ٥ ص ١٤٦.

[٥] الدارقطني، العلل، ج ٧ ص ٢٩٠.

[٦] ناقصة في الأصل واستدركاها من ف.

ولا يجوز في الزرع. وقد كان في خيبر[٧] النخل والشجر والزرع وعاملهم
٧٤ أ رسول الله صلى الله عليه وعلى آله | على الشطر من ذلك كلّه.

وقال أكثر العامّة من السلف بمثل قول أهل البيت صلوات الله عليهم ووافقوهم فيه في أنّ المزارعة بالنصف والثلث والربع وما اشترط المتزارعان من ذلك جائز، وأنّه لا يجوز أن تكرى الأرض بطعام معلوم ممّا يزرع فيها، وكذلك قال أهل البيت صلوات الله عليهم.

واكتراء الأرض بمال من العين معلوم جائز عند الجميع. وقد قيل إنّ النهي عن المخابرة إنّما هو أن يشترط ربّ الأرض على العامل فيها كيلا معلومًا ممّا تخرج. وذلك منهي عنه كما ذكرت قبل.

وكذلك كانوا يستأجرونها على عهد رسول الله صلى الله عليه وعلى آله لأنّه لم تكن عند القوم أموال وأكثر ما يتعاملون بالسلع وبالعروض. فنهى رسول الله صلى الله عليه وعلى آله عن استئجار الأرض ممّن يزرعها بكيل من
٧٤ ب الطعام | الذي تخرجه إذ كان ذلك غير معلوم أنّها تخرجه، إذ قد لا تخرج شيئًا.

---

[٧] الأصل: الخيبر، وفي ف: خيبر وهو الصحيح.

وقال آخرون: كانوا يشترطون شيئًا بعينه على المزارعين ممّا تنبت الأرض، فنهى رسول الله صلى الله عليه وعلى آله عن ذلك لأنّه قد تنبت ذلك ويتمّ وقد لا تنبت ولا يتمّ.

وقال آخرون: وكانوا يعطون الأرض بالثلث والربع وأشباه ذلك ويشترطون لما تخرجه جداول معلومة منها، فنهى رسول الله صلى الله عليه وعلى آله عن العقد على ذلك لأنّه مجهول لا يُدرى هل تخرج تلك الجداول شيئًا أو لا تخرجه، في وجوه مثل هذا كثيرة ذكروها لا تجوز عقد المزارعة عليها.

وقال آخرون: إنّما نهى رسول الله صلى الله عليه وعلى آله عن ذلك نهي تأديب لا نهي تحريم لما رأى من كثرة خصومتهم فيه. فالمزارعة على النصف والثلث والربع وما | تعاقد عليه المتزارعان[8] من ذلك جائزة. ٧٥ أ

وكراء الأرض بالعين والعروض وغير ما يُزْرَع فيها من الحبّ جائز. ولا يجوز أن تُستأجر بشيء ممّا تخرجه لأنّها قد تخرج وقد لا تخرج، وهذا هو الذي [جاء][9] النهي فيه.[10] وبهذا قال عامّة الصحابة والتابعين ومن بعدهم من أهل الفتيا المتقدّمين.

---

[8] الأصل: المزارعان وأثبتنا النصّ من ف وهو الصواب.

[9] ناقصة في الأصل واستدركناها من ف.

[10] القاضي النعمان، دعائم الإسلام، ج ٢ ص ٧٢ حيث أورد المحقق فيضي في حواشي تحقيقه هذا النص من ذات البيان من قوله: وكراء الأرض بالعين إلخ...

وكره ذلك بعض المتأخرين، وقال بعضهم: لا يجوز. وقد ذكرت قولهم في أوّل الباب. ومن خالف ما ثبت عن رسول الله وعن الأئمّة من ذرّيّته صلوات الله عليه وعليهم لم يُلتفَت إلى قوله.

ذكر بيان
النهي عن المحاقلة

الحقل الزرع الذي يكثر ورقه قبل أن تغلظ سوقه، يقال منه: أحقل الزرع.[١١]
والمحاقلة فيه المبايعة، وذلك أن يباع في مثل هذه الحال قبل أن يبدو صلاحه، على أن يبقى في الأرض إلى أن يتمّ ويُحْصَد. فنهى رسول | الله ٧٥ ب صلى الله عليه وعلى آله عن ذلك وعن بيع كلّ ثمرة قبل أن يبدو صلاحها، لأنّ البيع في ذلك يقع على كلّ مجهول.
فإنْ بيع الزرع كذلك على أن يحصد قصبًا فلا بأس ببيعه لأنّ البيع وقع على معلوم منه غير مجهول.
[الزرع الأخضر إذا بيع على أن يحصد بحاله فذلك جائز، وإذا بيع على أن يتمّ ويحصد فذلك غير جائز].[١٢] [هذا قول أهل البيت صلوات الله عليهم]،[١٣] ووافقهم عليه أكثر أهل الفتيا من العامّة.

[١١] هكذا فسّره الجوهري بلفظه. راجع: الجوهري، الصحاح، مادّة ح ق ل.

[١٢] هذه الفقرة ناقصة من الأصل، واستدركناها (حتى قوله: غير جائز...) من حواشي المحقق فيضي على دعائم الإسلام حيث ينقلها من ذات البيان حسب قوله. إلا أنّ هذه الفقرة بعينها لم ترد في نسخة فيضي التي نعتمدها ولا ندري من أين أثبتها المحقق. راجع: القاضي النعمان، دعائم الإسلام، ج ٢ ص ٢٧.

[١٣] ناقصة في الأصل واستدركناها من ف.

وقال قوم منهم: المحاقلة كراء الأرض لتزرع بطعام ممّا تخرجه، وقد ذكرت أنّ ذلك غير جائز في الباب الذي قبل هذا الباب.

وقال آخرون: المحاقلة بيع الزرع بحنطة مكيلة، وهذا أيضًا غير جائز.

ذكر بيان
النهي عن المزابنة

المزابنة بيع التمر في رؤوس النخل بكيل من التمر، والعنب في الكرم بزبيب، وأشباه ممّا تباع في شجرة الثمرة بمثلها ممّا قد جمع.[١٤]

نهى رسول الله صلى الله عليه وعلى آله عن ذلك لأنّه لا يجوز بيع ذلك إلا مثلا بمثل من كلّ ما يُكال أو يوزن. وإذا بيع ذلك على رؤوس النخل بتمر مكيل، لم يعلم هل هو مثله | أو يزيد أو ينقص عنه، فنهى رسول الله صلى ٧٦ أ
الله عليه وعلى آله عن ذلك.

ورخّص في العرايا، والعريّة النخلة يعريها الرجل، أي يعطي ثمرتها [للآخر]،[١٥] ورخّص في بيعها بتمر لأنّهم شكوا إليه صلى الله عليه وعلى آله أنّ كثيرًا منهم يشتهي الرطب وليس عنده ما يشتريه [به][١٦] غير التمر، فرخّص من ذلك في مثل النخلة والنخلتين وهي العرايا.

ونهى عمّا سوى ذلك أن يباع إلا مثلا بمثل وكيلا ووزنًا. وهذا قول أهل البيت صلوات الله عليهم، ووافقهم عليه سائر العوامّ.

---

[١٤] راجع: القاضي النعمان، دعائم الإسلام، ج ٢ ص ٢٥.

[١٥] ناقصة في الأصل واستدركاها من ف.

[١٦] ناقصة في الأصل واستدركاها من ف.

ذكر بيان
النهي عن المعاومة[١٧]

هذا خبر مجمل روته العامّة عن رسول الله صلى الله عليه وعلى آله أنّه نهى عن بيع السنين.[١٨] وفي بعض الروايات: عن بيع المعاومة.[١٩] وفسّروا ذلك فقالوا: هو أن يبيع الرجل ثمرة نخلة أو شجرة لسنين لما يستقبل. قالوا: فلذلك نهى رسول الله صلى الله عليه وعلى آله عن بيع السنين وعن
٧٦ ب المعاومة، أي بيع الأعوام على | ما ذكرته.

وأجمع المنسوبون إلى الفقه من العامّة على ذلك من تأويلهم لهذا الخبر بآرائهم.

وكذلك يقول أهل البيت صلوات الله عليهم[٢٠] في أنّ من باع ثمرة نخلة أو شجرة قبل أن يبدو، أو قد بدا ولم يبدُ صلاحه، وذلك أن يزهو أو بعضه، وزهوه أن يحمرّ أو يصفرّ أو يبدو أطنابه، فإن باعه قبل ذلك لتلك السنة التي هو فيها أوّلها ولما بعدها، أو لم تكن أثمرت بعد فبيع، ذلك كلّه باطل لا

---

[١٧] الأصل: المعاملة، وأثبتنا النصّ من ف وهو الصواب.
[١٨] الشافعي، كتاب الأمّ، ج ٤ ص ١٣.
[١٩] مسلم، الصحيح، ج ٥ ص ١٩.
[٢٠] القاضي النعمان، دعائم الإسلام، ج ٢ ص ٢٤–٢٥.

يجوز لأنّ رسول الله صلى الله عليه وعلى آله نهى عن بيع الثمار قبل أن يبدو صلاحها. فبيع ذلك غير جائز على بائعه ولا على مشتريه إذا تنازعا فيه. وإن اتّفقا عليه ولم يتخاصما فليس ذلك بمحرّم. وإنّما نهى رسول الله صلى الله عليه وعلى آله لكثرة ما [كانوا][21] يختصمون في ذلك إذا اشتروه قبل أن يبدو صلاحه ثمّ أصابته جائحة، فنهاهم أن يبيعوه حتى يبدو صلاحه. فإن بدا صلاح شيء منه دون أن يكون قد بدا | صلاحه [كلّه][22] جاز بيعه. ٧٧ أ
وذلك إجماع لا اختلاف فيه.

وإذا باع بائع ذلك وقد بدا صلاحه أو صلاح بعضه لتلك السنة التي هو فيها، ولا يخرج منها بعدها لسنين، فذلك جائز في قول أهل البيت صلوات الله عليهم وغير جائز عند جميع العامّة. وهذا ممّا فارقوهم فيه بأسرهم لغلبة الجهل على جميعهم.

وهم يجيزون كلّهم بيع الثمرة إذا بدا صلاح بعضها ويروون أنّ رسول الله صلى الله عليه وعلى آله نهى عن بيع الثمرة قبل أن يبدو صلاحها، ويقولون: إذا بدا صلاح بعضها [جاز بيعها]،[23] ووقع البيع على ما بدا صلاحه منها، ويكون ما لم يبدُ صلاحه من ذلك تبعًا لما بدا صلاحه. وكذلك ما لم يخرج بعد

[21] ناقصة في الأصل واستدركناها من ف.

[22] ناقصة في الأصل واستدركناها من ف.

[23] ناقصة في الأصل واستدركناها من ف.

منه ممّا يكون بطونا من الثمار كالمقاثى والتين وأشباه ذلك، فهم يجيزون بيعه، ويجعلون ما لم يَزْهُ منه ويَبْدُ من صلاحه، أو ما لم يخرج بعد وكان
٧٧ ب مغيبًا منه، تبعًا | له وممّا يقع البيع عليه. ولا فرق بين ذلك وبين ما يأتي بعد السنة للسنين التي اشترطها المتبايعان إذا كان البيع قد وقع على ما زها وبدا صلاحه[٢٤] فيكون ما لم يظهر أو لم يَزْهُ تبعًا له.

وكما قد أجمعوا على ذلك من قولهم الذي حكيته عنهم، فيما يكون في العام إن لم تخرج في السنة أخرجت في الأخرى. وإن لم تخرج لما يستقبل كان البيع قد وقع على ما يجوز بيعه فيها ممّا زها وبدا صلاحه. كما لو قد هلك ما لم يَبْدُ صلاحه منه، أو لم تخرج ما يُنتَظر من باقي بطونه في العام الذي بيع ذلك فيه، لكان البيع صحيحًا عند العامّة الذين أنكروا ذلك للسنين، ووقع البيع عندهم على ما زها منه. ولا فرق في ذلك بين السنة الواحدة والسنين الكثيرة.

وقول رسول الله صلى الله عليه وعلى آله الذي رووه نهى عن بيع السنين، إذا
٧٨ أ ثبت عنه، لم ينبغ أن يتأوّلوه بآرائهم ولا أن | يأخذوا بيانه إلا من قِبَل الرسول عليه السلام الذي أمره الله عزّ وجلّ بالبيان، فقال: ﴿وَأَنزَلْنَا إِلَيْكَ الذِّكْرَ لِتُبَيِّنَ

---

[٢٤] الأصل: صلاحها وأُثبتنا النصّ من ف وهو الصواب.

لِلنَّاسِ مَا نُزِّلَ إِلَيْهِمْ﴾ ،[٢٥] والذي جاء عن الأئمّة من أهل بيته صلوات الله عليه وعليهم أجمعين ، فعنه أخذوه. وقد أبانوا عنه عليه وعليهم التحيّة والسلام أنّ الذي نُهِيَ عنه من بيع السنين وبيع المعاومة أن يباع ذلك قبل أن يبدو صلاح بعض ما يباع من الثمار لهذه السنين في حين عقد البيع على ذلك، أو لا تكون فيها ثمرة في حين عقد هذا البيع ، فهذا بيع لا يجوز بإجماع.

فكان الأولى بمن قال في بيان ذلك برأيه من العوامّ أن يأخذه عنهم عن الرسول عليه وعليهم السلام.

و[هذا][٢٦] ممّا أجمعوا أيضًا عليه معهم فيه دون أن يخالفوهم باستنباط يستنبطونه من قبل أنفسهم ويتأوّلونه على رسول الله صلى الله عليه وعلى آله ويثبتون به حكمًا ينسبونه إلى الله جلّ ذكره | ويجعلونه من أحكام دينه ٧٨ ب
الذي تعبّد به عباده من غير ردّ منهم ما جهلوه من ذلك إلى من أمروا بردّه إليه. نسأل الله العصمة من الخلاف والزيغ ونرغب إليه في الثبات على الهدى والحقّ برحمته.

ومثل هذا كان أولى بابن قتيبة أن ينبّه عليه من أراد تعليمه وإرشاده كما زعم، لو هُدي وأُرشد إلى حظه، لا أن يرمي له بالنكت التي رماها ممّا ذكره

---

[٢٥] النحل ١٦/٤٤.

[٢٦] ناقصة في المخطوطتين ولا يتمّ الكلام إلا بها.

من الفقه، ويزعم له أنّ [علم][٢٧] هذا يغنيه عن علم غيره من تطويل الفقهاء، إذا لم يجد بدًّا من ذكر ذلك في كتابه لئلا يقال إنه ضرب عن ذكر العلم صفحًا. وقد شرط في أوّله أن يدلّ من أراد تقويمه وتعليمه على فنون ممّا يرى أنّه يلزمه، فنبذ له هذه النبذ المجملة ثمّ أعلمه أنها تغنيه عن سائر العلوم الفقهيّة، لئلا يتعلق بطلبها[٢٨] فيعلم عواره وتخلفه عنها كما ذلك من علم طرفا منها.[٢٩]

٧٩ أ تمّ الجزء الثامن من | ذات البيان

والحمد لله ربّ العالمين.

يتلوه في الجزء التاسع

ذكر بيان النهي عن ربح ما لم تضمن وبيع ما لم تقبض

---

[٢٧] ناقصة في الأصل واستدركناها من ف.

[٢٨] الأصل: يتعلق بعوارها، وأثبتنا النصّ من ف وهو أصحّ.

[٢٩] نلاحظ أن القاضي النعمان قد أغفل هنا حديثا أورده ابن قتيبة في مقدّمة أدب الكاتب وهو: [النهي عن] بيع الثنية. ولعله أغفله لأنّ مقتضاه يظهر بتمامه في حديث النهي عن بيع الغرر الذي سيعالجه فيما بعد.

الجزء التاسع من ذات البيان

من تأليف القاضي النعمان بن محمد

قدّس الله روحه ورزقنا شفاعته وأنسه

بحقّ محمد وآله الطيّبين الطاهرين

صلوات الله عليهم أجمعين

| ذكر بيان ٦٩ ب

النهي عن ربح ما لم تضمن وبيع ما لم تقبض

ذكر ابن قتيبة أنّ هذا الخبر ممّا جاء عن رسول الله صلى الله عليه وعلى آله أنّه نهى عن ربح ما لم تضمن وبيع ما لم تقبض.

وقد روى هذا الحديث قوم من العامّة عن عمرو بن شعيب بن محمد بن عبد الله بن عمرو بن العاص[١] عن أبيه عن جدّه عن النبيّ صلى الله عليه وعلى آله أنّه قال: لا يحلّ بيع وسلف ولا شرطان في بيع ولا ربح ما لم تضمن وبيع ما

[١] عمرو بن شعيب بن محمد بن عبد الله بن عمرو بن العاص القرشي السهمي، أبو إبراهيم/أبو عبد الله المدني المتوفى ١١٨ هـ. راجع عنه: ابن حجر، تهذيب التهذيب، ج ٦ ص ١٥٩ – ١٦٤.

ليس عندك.[٢] وحديث عمرو بن شعيب عن أبيه عن جدّه عن النبيّ صلى الله عليه وعلى آله عند العامّة لا يثبت وهو ضعيف عندهم، وقالوا: إنّما كان يحدّث من كتاب، فيقول: حدّثني أبي عن جدّي.[٣]

ورووا أيضًا بعض هذا الحديث من طريق يوسف بن ماهك[٤] عن حكيم بن حزام، وهو منقطع لأنّ بينهما عبد الله بن عصمة،[٥] وقد أدخل بينهما[٦] بعضهم عليّ بن حكيم، أنّ رسول الله صلى الله عليه وعلى آله قال لحكيم
٨٠أ بن حزام:[٧] ألم أنبأ، أو، ألم يبلغني،[٨] أو كما شاء الله، أنّك | تبيع طعامًا؟ قال حكيم: قلت: بلى يا رسول الله. قال: فلا تبيعن طعاما حتى تشتريه وتستوفيه. وروى بعض الشيعة [أيضًا][٩] هذا الحديث من طريق زيد بن

---

[٢] راجع الحديث بهذا الإسناد: عبد الرزاق، المصنف، ج ٨ ص ٣٩.

[٣] راجع عن ذلك: ابن حجر، تهذيب التهذيب، ج ٦ ص ١٦١– ١٦٢.

[٤] يوسف بن ماهك بن مهران الفارسي المكي المتوفى ١٠٣ هـ. راجع عنه: ابن حجر، تهذيب التهذيب، ج ٩ ص ٤٤٢.

[٥] عبد الله بن عصمة الجُشمي. لم يذكر تأريخ وفاته. راجع عنه: ابن حجر، تهذيب التهذيب، ج ٤ ص ٣٩٩– ٤٠٠.

[٦] الأصل: بينهم، وأثبتنا النصّ من ف وهو أصحّ.

[٧] راجع عن هذه الروايات بأسانيدها: الشافعي، الرسالة، ص ٣٣٥– ٣٣٧. ويبدو أن القاضي النعمان نقلها من هذا المصدر.

[٨] الأصل: لم، وأثبتنا النصّ من ف وهو أصحّ.

[٩] ناقصة في الأصل واستدركناها من ف.

عليّ بن الحسين عن آبائه عن عليّ عليه السلام أنّ رسول الله صلى الله عليه وعلى آله نهى عن ربح ما لم تضمَن،[١٠] وهذه [الرواية][١١] كرواية العامّة.

وقد اختلفوا في تأويل النهي عن ربح ما لم تضمن وبيع ما لم تقبض، فقال بعضهم: لا يكون ذلك إلا في الطعام خاصة أن يبيعه قبل أن يقبضه.

وقال آخرون: ليس ذلك في العموم، وإنّما هو خاصّ من البيوع، ومعناه أن يبيع شيئاً بعينه وليس ذلك الشيء عنده. قالوا: والدليل على ذلك إجماع المسلمين على السلم، وهو بيع طعام معلوم أو ما وقع السلم عليه ممّا يُكال أو يوزن أو يوصف بصفة معلومة، وليس ذلك عند البائع في وقت عقد السلم، وهو بيعه. والسلم جائز بإجماع، وقد رخّص فيه رسول الله صلى الله عليه وعلى آله.

وكذلك قد أجمعوا على ربح ما لم تضمن من جهة [أخرى]،[١٢] وهو | ٨٠ب
المضارب يعمل بمال الرجل على أنّه ما ربح فيه كان له نصفه، ولا ضمان عليه فيه إن هلك أو شيئاً[١٣] منه. فدلّ ذلك على أنّ النهي عن بيع ما ليس عندك وربح ما لم تضمن إنّما هو شيء دون شيء، مثل بيع الرجل ما لم

---

[١٠] راجع لرواية زيد بن علي: مسند زيد، ص ٢٥٩– ٢٦٠.

[١١] ناقصة في الأصل واستدركناها من ف.

[١٢] ناقصة في المخطوطتين ويقتضيها سياق الكلام.

[١٣] في المخطوطتين: شيء منه، ولعلّ ما اثبتناه هو الصحيح.

يملكه وهو في ملك غيره، وربح ما لم تضمن وهو استئجار الغلام أو الدار أو الدابّة أو قبالة العمل بأجر، ثم يُؤجّر ذلك بأكثر منه ولم يضمن ذلك ولا عمل فيه ولا عني. فإن عني فيه أو عمل طاب له الربح. وهذا والذي قبله لا يجوز بيعه ولا الفضل فيه عند أهل البيت صلوات الله عليهم.

وقالوا: وبيع الطعام قبل أن يقبض لا يجوز بالربح ولا بالخسران. فعلمنا أنّ العلة لو كانت في الطعام لجاز بيعه بالخسران لأنّ النهي إنّما جاء عن الربح [فيه][4] خاصّة، وقد أجمعوا أنّ بيع الطعام قبل أن يقبض لا يجوز بالربح ولا بالخسران.

والحديث كما ذكرناه معلول ليس يُحْتَجّ به في كلّ شيء، وبيان علته، وأنّه
٨١أ ليس يجري في كلّ شيء ذكرته من إجازة السلم والمضاربة بإجماع، | وفيهما بيع ما ليس عند البائع وربح ما لم يضمنه المضارب.

ولكن قد يُنهى عن بيع ما ليس عند البائع وربح ما لم يضمنه الرابح في وجوه، ولا يجوز بعض ذلك بإجماع. وقد يجوز بعضه عند قوم ولا يجوز عند قوم. ولو كان هذا الحديث صحيحًا لقضى على ما فيه الإجماع والاختلاف من ذلك ولم يكونوا ليجمعوا على خلاف حديث ثابت عن رسول الله صلى الله عليه وعلى آله يجري مجرى العموم.

---

[4] ناقصة في الأصل واستدركناها من ف.

فممّا يدخل في جملة النهي بإجماع عن بيع ما ليس عندك، بيع كلّ محرم كبيع الأحرار والميتة والدم ولحم الخنزير والخمر وكلّ ما يحرم ملكه، لأنّ بائع ذلك يبيع ما لا يملكه، إذ لا يملك المرء ما حُرّم عليه أن يملكه، ولا يكون ذلك في الحقيقة عنده وإن كان في يديه.

ومن ذلك أيضا بيع الغرر، وقد نهى عنه رسول الله صلى الله عليه وعلى آله،[١٥] وهو كلّ بيع عقده المتبايعان على شيء مجهول عند البائع والمشتري أو عند أحدهما. فمن ذلك | بيع ما في بطون الحيوان من الأنعام والبهائم، ٨١ ب وبيع الألبان في ضروع الأنعام، وبيع السمن في الألبان، وعصير عنب بعينه، [وعصير زيتون بعينه]،[١٦] وبيع الحيتان في الماء التي لا تؤخذ إلا بالصيد، وبيع الطائر في السماء كذلك، وبيع العبد الآبق والبعير الشارد وكلّ شيء معدوم الشخص في وقت عقد البيع عليه. وإن وُجد وُجد مجهولا، يقلّ ويكثر، وما كان في هذا المعنى وهو كثير يطول ذكره ويخرج عن حدّ هذا الكتاب، وقد ذكرته فيما صنّفته من كتب الفقه في أبواب البيوع مطوّلا فيما أشبعته، ومختصرًا فيما اختصرته، وكذلك وجوه تجري عليه يخرج استقصاؤها أيضا عن حدّ هذا الكتاب. من ذلك أنّ ما ذكرته هاهنا من بيع

---

[١٥] راجع: الشافعي، الأم، ج ٧ ص ٣٠٥؛ الطوسي، الخلاف، ج ٣ ص ٥٣.

[١٦] ناقصة في الأصل واستدركناها من ف.

هذه المبيعات إذا بيع مع شيء حاضر معلوم جاز عند أهل البيت صلوات الله عليهم بيعه، ويقع البيع على الحاضر من ذلك ويكون الغائب تبعًا له، كما يقع
البيع على الثمرة إذا زها بعضها ولم يزه[١٧] أكثرها.[١٨] وقد نهى رسول | الله صلى ٨٢أ
اله عليه وعلى آله عن بيع الثمار [حتى تزهو]،[١٩] وغير ذلك من نظائر هذا كثير.

وأمّا ما اختلفوا في ملكه وبيعه، فمثل الكلب العقور والهرّ وأشباه ذلك ممّا يطول أيضًا ذكره ويخرج عن حدّ هذا الكتاب استقصاؤه وذكر الاختلاف فيه والثابت الصحيح عن أهل البيت صلوات الله عليهم منه. وكذلك يجري مثل ذلك في أبواب كثيرة من أبواب ما نُهي عنه وأبواب ما نُهي عن بيعه، لو استقصيتها لانقطع هذا الكتاب [بذكرها][٢٠] عمّا بُني عليه، وبعضها يجري ذكره فيه. ومن أراد استقصاءها وجدها حيث ذكرته من كتب الفقه إن شاء الله.

---

[١٧] الأصل: أو يزه أكثرها، وأثبتنا النصّ من ف وهو الصواب.

[١٨] راجع لهذه المسألة: القاضي النعمان، دعائم الإسلام، ج ٢ ص ٢٤.

[١٩] ناقصة في الأصل واستدركناها من ف.

[٢٠] ناقصة في الأصل واستدركناها من ف.

وهذا أيضًا ممّا يدخل على ابن قتيبة فيما زعم أنه يُكتفى به ممّا ذكره[٢١] من هذه الجمل عن تطويل الفقهاء. وهذا مختصر من تطويل لولاه لم يكن لمعرفة قوله: وكنهيه - يعني رسول الله صلى الله عليه وعلى آله - عن ربح ما لم تضمن وبيع ما لم تقبض، فائدة أكثر من تطلّب علم ذلك وبيانه من تطويل الفقهاء الذي زعم أنّه يُستغنى عنه، | و[ما][٢٢] يُستغنى عن ذلك إلا بالجهل ٨٢ب الذي استغنى هو به عن أمثاله ممّا لا يسع جهله ولا ينبغي إلا طلبه ومعرفته.

---

[٢١] الأصل: مما ذكرته، وأثبتنا النصّ من ف وهو أصحّ.

[٢٢] ناقصة في الأصل واستدركناها من ف.

ذكر بيان

النهي عن بيعتين في بيعة وشرطين في بيع

هذا خبر ثابت عن رسول الله صلى الله عليه وعلى آله أنّه نهى عن بيعتين في بيعة وشرطين في بيع.[٢٣] وروى كثير من العامّة ذلك عن رسول الله صلى الله عليه وعلى آله بمثل هذا اللفظ،[٢٤] وما هو في معناه مثل: صفقتين في صفقة وشرطين في شرط.[٢٥]

واختلفوا في تأويل ذلك، فقال بعضهم: هو أن يقول: أبيعك هذه السلعة نقدًا بكذا ونسيئة بكذا، ويتعاقدان البيع على ذلك على أنّه أيّهما أتى المشتري كان البيع عليه.

وقال آخرون: هو أن يقول له: أبيعك هذه السلعة بكذا من الدنانير على أن تعطيني بها دراهم من صرف كل دينار منها بكذا وكذا، أو بدراهم على أن تعطيني دنانير بصروفها، صرف كلّ دينار منها بكذا وكذا درهم إلى أجل كذا
٨٣أ بعد محل الدنانير والدراهم، ويتعاقدان على البيع على ذلك. | قالوا: فهذا من

---

[٢٣] الشافعي، الأم، ج ٣ ص ٣٤؛ الطوسي، الخلاف، ج ٢ ص ١٥٩.

[٢٤] مالك بن أنس، الموطأ، ج ٢ ص ٦٦٣–٦٦٤.

[٢٥] السرخسي، المبسوط، ج ١٢ ص ١٦٣.

بيعتين في بيعة وشرطين في شرط وصرف عين بورق إلى أجل. وكلّ ذلك غير جائز.

قالوا: ومن ذلك أن يقول الرجل: ابتَع منّي كذا من جزاف أو كيل [بكذا][٢٦] على أن تبيعني كذا بكذا، حاضرًا كان ذلك أو غائبًا، مضمونًا أو غير مضمون، فذلك من بيعتين في بيعة. وهذا كلّه من البيوع فاسد لا يجوز عند أهل البيت صلوات الله عليهم. ووافقهم عليه أكثر أهل الفتيا من العامّة.

وشذّ بعضهم فقال: يجوز البيع على أن يعقد على النقد بكذا والنسيئة بكذا ما لم يفترقا. فإن افترقا على ذلك فالبيع بأقلّ الثمنين إلى أبعد الأجلين. وهذا خلاف لما جاء عن رسول الله صلى الله عليه وعلى آله وعقد مجهول غير جائز عند عامّة أهل الفتيا.

[٢٦] ناقصة في الأصل واستدركناها من ف.

ذكر بيان
النهي عن بيع وسلف

هذا خبر ثابت عن رسول الله صلى الله عليه وعلى آله، رواه أهل البيت صلوات الله عليهم عنه عليه السلام، أنّه نهى عن بيع وسلف.[٢٧] وروى ذلك كثير من أصحاب الحديث من العامّة بمثل هذا اللفظ.[٢٨]

واختلفوا في تأويله، فقال | قوم: هو أن يقول الرجل للرجل: أبتاع منك ٨٣ب
سلعتك بكذا وكذا على أن تسلفني إلى أجل كذا وكذا.

وقال آخرون: هو أن يقرضه قرضًا ثم يبايعه على ذلك. وكلا الوجهين عند أهل البيت صلوات الله عليهم يدخل في النهي عن بيع وسلف وما أشبه ذلك، لأنّ منفعة السلف غير معلومة، وإذا كان ذلك العقد على مجهول وصار منهيًّا عنه من وجه آخر – وهو نهي رسول الله صلى الله عليه وعلى آله – عن سلف يجرّ منفعة.

ومن ذلك ما سأل عنه أبا عبد الله جعفر بن محمد صلوات الله عليهما بعضُ أوليائه فقال: جُعلت فداك، أُعطي الرجل له الثمرة الدنانير سلفًا وأقول له: هذه الدنانير لي عليك على أنّ ثمرتك إذا زهت وقامت للبيع بما تقوم عليه إن

---

[٢٧] القاضي النعمان، دعائم الإسلام، ج ٢ ص ٣٣.
[٢٨] مالك بن أنس، الموطأ، ج ٢ ص ٦٨٥.

شئتُ أخذتُ وإن شئتُ تركتُ. فقال له: أما تستطيع أن تعطيه ولا تشترط شيئًا؟ قال: جعلت [فداك][29] فإن الله يعلم أنّ ذلك من نيّتي. قال: إذا كان
ذلك من نيّتك فلا خير فيه، إمّا أن تسلفه سلفًا بلا شرط ابتياع | شيء منه ١٨٤أ
وإمّا أن تدع ذلك فتشتري بما تتّفقان عليه في [وقت][30] عقدة البيع.[31]

وسأله رجل آخر عن رجل ابتاع سلعة بمائة دينار على أن يسلفه البائع مائة دينار، فقال: ينقض هذا البيع إلا أن يشاء المشتري ردّ المائة دينار التي تسلف منه ويمضي البيع، فإن انتفع المشتري بالذي تسلف فسخ البيع بينهما.

قال السائل: فإن أسلف رجل رجلا دنانير ثمّ لقيه بعد ذلك فسأله أن يبيع منه وينظره ويكون عليه ما أسلفه لمن باعه من غير شرط عند السلف، ما حاله؟ قال: لا بأس بذلك.[32]

---

[29] ناقصة في الأصل واستدركناها من ف.

[30] ناقصة في الأصل واستدركناها من ف.

[31] الكليني، الكافي، ج ٥ ص ١٧٧.

[32] لم أعثر على هذا الحديث بهذا اللفظ فيما بين يدي من مصادر. وقارن بكلام الشافعي، كتاب الأم، ج ٣ ص ٣٨.

ذكر بيان
النهي عن بيع الغرر وبيع المواصفة

قد تقدّم ذكر بيع الغرر في بيان النهي عن ربح ما لم تضمن وبيع ما لم تقبض، وبيع المواصفة منه. وهو أن يقول: أبيعك سلعة أو ضيعة أو عبدًا[٣٣] أو أمة أو ثوبًا أو طعامًا أو ما كان، ويصفه له – ولا يراه المشتري – بكذا وكذا نقد، ويتعاقدان البيع على ذلك ويفترقان | عليه، فذلك بيع فاسد. والمشتري ٨٤ب
بخيار النظر إذا رأى ذلك المبيع، إن شاء أخذه وإن شاء تركه. وكذلك البائع له أن يرجع فيه لأنّه انعقد على غير معلوم. ولا يجوز مثل هذا[٣٤] إلا في السلم فيما يجوز فيه السلف. وذكر ذلك يطول ويخرج عن حدّ هذا الكتاب، وهو مذكور في أبواب السلم من أبواب البيوع في كتب الفقه. فإنّ ذلك يجوز بيعه بالصفة إذا عقد على أربعة شروط: (١) وذلك أن يوصف بصفة معلومة، (٢) ويُذكر قبضه إلى أجل معلوم، (٣) ويكون ذلك الذي وقع عليه السلم موجودًا في ذلك الوقت، وإن كان غير موجود فيه بطل السلم وكان من بيع ما ليس عندك، وأن يدفع المشتري الثمن، فإن لم يدفعه كان من باب

[٣٣] الأصل: عبيد، وأثبتنا النصّ من ف وهو أجود.
[٣٤] كتبت العبارة "مثل هذا" في الهامش بنفس الخط.

الكالئ بالكالئ، وسنذكره، (٤) ويذكر المكان الذي يكون القبض فيه. فبيع المواصفة على هذا يجوز ولا يجوز في غيره، وذلك إجماع فيما علمت والله أعلم.

وإذا أقرّ المشتري أنه قد عرف ذلك جاز | البيع عليه، وإن كان إنّما عرف ١٨٥أ
ذلك بصفة من وصفه له، وعلى هذا يكتب الناس وثائق البيوع.

وأكثر من يشتري أكثر الرباع وغيرها ولا يراها وإنّما توصف له، فإن أقرّ أنّه قد عرفها مضى البيع عليه. وإن لم يقرّ بذلك، وكان إنّما وصفت له ولم يقل عند عقد الشراء إنّه قد عرفها، لم ينعقد البيع وكان ذلك بيع المواصفة المنهي عنه.

وكذلك إن كان البائع لا يعرف أيضًا ما باعه إلا بالصفة لم يجز البيع عليه حتى يقرّ أنّه قد عرف ما باعه. والمعرفة قد تكون بالخبر وبالصفة وبالعيان وبالسماع وبغير ذلك من الحواسّ. ولذلك كتب الموثقون إقرار المشتري والبائع بمعرفة ما تبايعاه.

ذكر بيان قوله:
النهي عن الكالئ بالكالئ

هذا خبر روي عن رسول الله صلى الله عليه وآله أنّه نهى عن الكالئ بالكالئ أي الدَين بالدين. يقال منه: تكلأت كلأة[٣٥] إذا استنسأت شيئًا، والنسيئة التأخير.[٣٦] ويقال في الدعاء: بلغ الله بك أكلأ العمر أي آخره | وأبعده، وهو ٨٥ب
من التأخير.[٣٧]

والدين بالدين غير جائز عند أهل البيت صلوات الله عليهم. ووافقهم على ذلك المنسوبون إلى الفتيا من العامّة.

ومن ذلك أن يسلم الرجل إلى الرجل دنانير على طعام إلى أجل ولا يحضر الطعام عند من هو عليه، فيشتريه ممن وجب له إلى [أجل][٣٨] آخر بمال معلوم. فهذا دين انقلب إلى دين مثله وسلف بسلف.

---

[٣٥] في المخطوطتين: تكلأت كلاء ولا يصحّ، وأثبتنا عبارة معجم مقاييس اللغة لابن فارس (ج ٥ ص ١٣٢) ولسان العرب وتاج العروس، مادة ك ل ء.

[٣٦] راجع: أبو عبيد، غريب الحديث، ج ١ ص ٢٠. وقد نقل القاضي النعمان هذه العبارة حرفيا. راجع أيضا: القاضي النعمان، دعائم الإسلام، ج ٢ ص ٣٣.

[٣٧] وهذه العبارة أيضا منقولة من المصدر المذكور أعلاه، راجع: أبو عبيد، غريب الحديث، ج ١ ص ٢١.

[٣٨] ناقصة في الأصل واستدركناها من ف.

ومن ذلك أن يسلم الرجل في سلم معلوم على مال معلوم على أن يكون المال باقيًا عليه. فذلك لا يجوز لأنّه يصير دينًا بدين.

وقد ذكرت في الباب الذي قبل هذا الباب ما يجوز عليه عقد السلم، والسلم سلف. ومثل هذا كثير. منه ما سئل عنه الصادق جعفر بن محمد صلوات الله عليه عن رجل صانع عليه لرجل دين فدفع إليه عملا ليعمله له به، قال: لا يصلح ذلك لأنّه دين بدين، ولكن يدفع إليه ما له عليه ويقبضه ذلك في أجرته.

قال: وكذلك إن اكترى رجل من رجل ظهرًا بشيء معلوم فأحاله بذلك على رجل له عليه | دين، فذلك لا يصلح لأنه دين بدين. ١٨٦أ

قال: وكذلك الشريكان يكون لهما الدين فيريدان أن يتقاسما ويصير لكلّ واحد منهما منه شيء على من هو عليه، قال: لا يصلح ذلك لأنّه [ذمّة][39] بذمّة، وما اقتضاه كلّ واحد منهما فهو بينهما، وما هلك من ذلك فهو عليهما.[40]

ومثل هذا كثير يطول ذكره، وهو مذكور في موضعه من كتب الفقه، مبسوط في أبواب البيوع. فمن أراد معرفته وجده هناك إن شاء الله.

---

[39] ناقصة في الأصل واستدركناها من ف.

[40] أورد القاضي النعمان بعض هذه المسائل في دعائم الإسلام، ج ٢ ص ٣٤–٣٥.

ذكر النهي عن تلقي الركبان

الحديث ثابت عن رسول الله صلى الله عليه وآله أنّه نهى عن تلقي الركبان.

روى ذلك أهل البيت صلوات الله عليهم عنه عليه السلام وجماعة من المنسوبين إلى الفتيا من العوامّ أنّه نهى عن تلقي الركبان وتلقي السلع وتلقي البيوع. وذلك أن يخرج من المصر أو السوق من يريد شراء ما يؤتى به إليه فيلقى الذين يجلبون ذلك بعيدًا بحيث لا يكون جماعة ممن يريد شراء ذلك،
٨٦ب فيشتريه منهم. فنهى عن ذلك لما يدخله من البخس على | البائع، لأنّه قد لا يعلم السعر، وعلى المشترين الذين لم يخرجوا، لما يحرمون من الشراء.

وحدّ أهل البيت صلوات الله عليهم في ذلك مسافة غدوة أو روحة، وذلك مثل بريد فما دونه، والبريد اثنا عشر ميلا. فمن اشترى فيما جاوز ذلك لم يدخل في حدّ النهي وكان كمن اشترى في البوادي والقرى. ويفسخ البيع فيما اشتريَ من ذلك عند أهل البيت صلوات الله عليهم في حدّ حدّوه لأنّه من الحدّ المنهي عنه، ووافقهم على ذلك فريق من العامّة.[٤١]

وقال آخرون: البيع جائز والبائع بالخيار إذا ورد السوق فإن شاء أمضاه وإن شاء فسخه.

---

[٤١] أورد القاضي النعمان هذه المسألة بلفظها كما هي هنا في مختصر الآثار. راجع حاشية المحقق فيضي، دعائم الإسلام، ج ٢ ص ٣١.

وقال آخرون: ذلك مكروه والبيع جائز.

وقال آخرون: البيع جائز ولم يذكروا كراهة ذلك، وقالوا: لا خيار فيه للبائع ولا للمشتري، وما نهى رسول الله صلى الله عليه وآله لم يجز استعماله.

[الخاتمة][1]

فهذا آخر المسائل التي ذكرها ابن قتيبة.

فأمّا قوله بعد ذكرها: في أشباه لهذا فكثير،[2] لو ذكرته مجملا كما ذكره لكان
٨٧ أ أضعاف ما حُكِيَ عنه و[أضعاف][3] أضعافه إلى ما يطول ويكثر. وليس | في قوله هذا فائدة لمن أراد بزعمه تعليمه إذ لم يوقفه عليه. مع أنّ قوله: أشباه لهذا، إنّما يقع على ما هو في معناه من مثل الأبواب التي ذكرها وأعرض عمّا هو من الفقه الذي ذكر أنّ ذلك منه ألزم منها ممّا ذكرنا ما يجب أن يُبْتَدَأَ بعلمه مما بدأ الله عزّ وجلّ من فرائضه على عباده التي ألزمهم إيّاها في حين البلوغ ووقت التكليف، من فرائض المعرفة بأوليائه والطهارة والصلاة والزكاة والصوم والحجّ [والجهاد]،[4] ثمّ التفقّه في الدين في أبواب الفقه.

وقد رتّب ذلك الفقهاء على مرتبة الأوّل فالأوّل على ما يجب أن يبتدئ المتعلم منه ممّا يلزمه علمه أوّلا فأوّلا، على ذلك بسطوا ما بسطوه من الكتب فيه إذ كان ذلك لا ينبغي إلا كذلك. فتعدّى ابن قتيبة بمن زعم أنّه أراد تعليمه

---

[1] ليست في المخطوطتين.

[2] عبارة ابن قتيبة في أدب الكاتب المطبوع، ص ١٤: وأشباه لهذا كثيرة. وراجع حاشية المحقق.

[3] ناقصة في الأصل واستدركناها من ف.

[4] ناقصة في الأصل واستدركناها من ف.

الفقه هذا الترتيب لجهله بالعلم وقصد إلى نكت مجملة بعيدة من حدّ المتعلم المبتدئ، فذكر له مجملها ووكله في علم بيانها ومعرفتها إلى نفسه بقوله | ٨٧ ب
بعد ذكرها - إذا هو حفظها وتفهّم معانيها وتدبّرها - أغنته بإذن الله عن كثير[٥] من إطالة الفقهاء. واقتصاره[٦] هو وأئمّته وأتباعهم في علم البيان وما لا يعلمون تأويله على أنفسهم، وتركهم ردّ ما أمرهم الله عزّ وجلّ بردّه إلى أولي الأمر الذين أمر بردّ ذلك إليهم، وتركهم سؤال أهل الذكر عمّا لا يعلمون الذين أمرهم الله عزّ وجلّ بسؤالهم عن ذلك، أغرقهم في الجهل وأبعدهم عن الهدى وأصمّهم وأعماهم. فعلى أصله في ذلك بنى قوله هذا وأمر به من زعم أنّه أراد تعليمه، وهو إلى أن يزيده بذلك جهلا أقرب.

وكيف يتفهّم من لا يعلم معاني ما جهله أو يتدبّره ولم يجعل الله عزّ وجلّ ذلك لأحد من خلقه ولا علم رسله منهم من العلم إلا ما علمهم كما قال جلّ من قائل لمحمد نبيّه صلى الله عليه وآله: ﴿وَعَلَّمَكَ مَا لَمْ تَكُنْ تَعْلَمُ وَكَانَ فَضْلُ اللَّهِ عَلَيْكَ عَظِيمًا﴾ [٧]، وقال: ﴿هُوَ الَّذِي بَعَثَ فِي الْأُمِّيِّينَ رَسُولاً مِّنْهُمْ يَتْلُو عَلَيْهِمْ آيَاتِهِ وَيُزَكِّيهِمْ وَيُعَلِّمُهُمُ الْكِتَابَ وَالْحِكْمَةَ وَإِن كَانُوامِن قَبْلُ لَفِي ضَلَالٍ

---

[٥] الأصل: كثيرة، وأثبتنا النصّ من ف وهو الصواب.
[٦] الأصل: ولاقتصاره، وأثبتنا النصّ من ف وهو أصحّ.
[٧] النساء ٤/١١٣.

مُّبِينٍ﴾.[٨] وقال رسول الله صلى الله عليه وآله: تعلموا من عالم أهل بيتي وممّن تعلم من عالم أهل بيتي.[٩] وإنّما أمر الله عزّ وجلّ بتعلم العلم من العلماء الذين علمهم عزّ وجلّ إيّاه وهم رسله الذين أوحى إليهم ومن أقاموه للأمم من بعدهم من أئمّتهم، لا أن يتعلم العباد ذلك ويتفهّموه ويتدبّروه من [قبل][١٠] أنفسهم ويستغنوا عن الفقهاء كما زعم هذا الجاهل بالعلم وحدوده ومراتبه وكيف ينبغي أخذه، فضلّ من أجل ذلك وأضلّ غيره. نسأل الله العصمة من الضلالة والسلامة من الزيغ عن الهدى والتوفيق إليه لنا ولجميع المؤمنين.

تمّت الرسالة بحمد الله وعونه ومادّة وليّه في أرضه عليه أسنا تحياته وسلامه ما دار الفلك في مقامه. والحمد لله ربّ العالمين وصلى الله على رسوله محمد خاتم النبيّين وعلى أبرار عترته الأئمّة الصادقين وسلم تسليمًا.
وحسبنا الله ونعم الوكيل ونعم المولى ونعم النصير ولا حول | ولا قوّة إلا بالله ٨٨ ب
العليّ العظيم.

---

[٨] الجمعة ٦٢/٢.

[٩] راجع: القاضي النعمان، دعائم الإسلام، ج ١ ص ٨٠. وأورد القاضي النعمان الحديث في الدعائم موقوفا عن جعفر الصادق بهذا النصّ: تعلموا من عالم أهل بيتي وممّن تعلم من علم أهل بيتي تنجوا من النار. أما النوري الطبرسي فقد أورد الحديث مرفوعا إلى النبيّ من طريق جعفر الصادق، راجع: النوري، مستدرك الوسائل، ج ١٧ ص ٢٤٤ وص ٢٧٢.

[١٠] ناقصة من الأصل واستدركناها من ف.

قد وقع الفراغ من هذه النسخة الشريفة بعون الله وحسن توفيقه ومادّة وليّه في أرضه سلام الله عليه وداعيه داعي الدعاة ومنبع البركات الشيخ محمد عزّ الهدى والدين خلد الله بقاءه أبد الآبدين ودهر الداهرين بمحمد وآله أجمعين في اليوم الثالث عشر من شهر رجب الأصب من سنة ١٢٣٣ في درس الداعي المذكور حفظه الله تعالى في بلدة سورت بندر حفظها الله تعالى.[١١]

---

[١١] هذه الخاتمة في الأصل فقط.

قائمة مراجع التحقيق

رتبنا هذه القائمة الألفبائية حسب المشهور المتداول من أسماء المؤلفين.

ابن أبي شيبة، المصنف

عبد الله بن محمد بن أبي شيبة. *المصنف في الأحاديث والآثار*. تحقيق سعيد اللحام. بيروت ١٩٨٩.

ابن حجر، تهذيب التهذيب

أحمد بن علي بن حجر العسقلاني. *تهذيب التهذيب*. ضبط ومراجعة صدقي جميل العطار. بيروت ١٩٩٥.

ابن قتيبة، أدب الكاتب

عبد الله بن مسلم بن قتيبة. *أدب الكاتب*. تحقيق محمد الدالي، بيروت ١٩٨٦.

ابن قتيبة، غريب الحديث

عبد الله بن مسلم بن قتيبة. *غريب الحديث*. تحقيق عبد الله الجبوري. بيروت ١٩٨٨.

ابن قتيبة، المعارف

عبد الله بن مسلم بن قتيبة. *كتاب المعارف*. تحقيق ثروة عكاشة، القاهرة ١٩٨١.

ابن قدامة، المغني

عبد الله بن أحمد بن مجمد بن قدامة. *المغني على مختصر الخرقي*. بيروت بدون تأريخ.

ابن كثير، تفسير

إسماعيل بن كثير. *تفسير القرآن العظيم*. بيروت ١٩٩٢.

ابن منظور، لسان العرب

محمد بن مكرم بن منظور. *لسان العرب*. قم ١٤٠٥ هـ.

أبو عبيد، غريب الحديث

أبو عبيد القاسم بن سلام. *غريب الحديث*. حيدر آباد ١٩٧٦.

أبو عبيدة، الديباج

أبو عبيدة معمر بن المثنى. *كتاب الديباج*. تحقيق عبد الله بن سليمان الجربوع وعبد الرحمن بن سليمان العثيمين. القاهرة ١٩٩١.

أحمد، مسند

أحمد بن حنبل. *المسند*. بيروت، بدون تأريخ.

الأصفهاني، الأغاني

أبو الفرج علي بن الحسين الأصفهاني. *كتاب الأغاني*. تحقيق سمير جابر. بيروت بدون تأريخ.

البيهقي، السنن الكبرى

احمد بن الحسين بن علي البيهقي. *السنن الكبرى*. بيروت بدون تأريخ.

الترمذي، السنن

محمد بن عيسى الترمذي. *سنن الترمذي*. تحقيق عبد الوهاب عبد اللطيف. بيروت ١٩٨٣.

الحاكم النيسابوري، المستدرك

محمد بن عبد الله الحاكم النيسابوري. *المستدرك على الصحيحين*. إشراف يوسف عبد الرحمن المرعشلي. بيروت بدون تأريخ.

الجوهري، الصحاح

إسماعيل بن حماد الجوهري. *تاج اللغة وصحاح العربية*. تحقيق أحمد عبد الغفور عطار. القاهرة، بيروت ١٩٨٤.

الحربي، غريب الحديث

إبراهيم بن إسحاق الحربي. *غريب الحديث*. تحقيق سليمان بن إبراهيم بن محمد العايز. جدة ١٩٨٥.

الخليل بن أحمد، العين

الخليل بن أحمد الفراهيدي. *كتاب العين*. تحقيق مهدي المخزومي وإبراهيم السامرائي. بيروت ١٩٨٨.

الدارقطني، سنن

علي بن عمر الدارقطني. *سنن الدارقطني*. تحقيق مجدي بن منصور بن سيد الشورى. بيروت ١٩٩٦.

الدارقطني، العلل

علي بن عمر الدارقطني. *العلل الواردة في الأحاديث النبوية*. تحقيق محفوظ الرحمن زين الله السلفي. الرياض ١٩٨٥.

الذهبي، سير

محمد بن أحمد بن عثمان الذهبي. *سير أعلام النبلاء*. تحقيق شعيب الأرنؤوط. بيروت ١٩٩٠.

الزبيدي، تاج العروس

محمد مرتضى الزبيدي. *تاج العروس من جواهر القاموس*. تحقيق علي شيري. بيروت ١٩٩٤.

زيد بن علي، المسند

زيد بن علي بن الحسين. *مسند زيد بن علي*. بيروت بدون تأريخ.

السرخسي، المبسوط

محمد بن أحمد السرخسي. *المبسوط*. بيروت ١٩٨٦.

السيوطي، الدر المنثور

عبد الرحمان بن أبي بكر السيوطي. *الدر المنثور في التفسير بالمأثور*. بيروت بدون تأريخ.

الشافعي، إختلاف الحديث

محمد بن إدريس الشافعي. *إختلاف الحديث*. تحقيق محمد أحمد عبد العزيز. بيروت ١٩٨٦.

الشافعي، الأم

محمد بن إدريس الشافعي. *كتاب الأم*. بيروت ١٩٨٠.

الشافعي، الرسالة

محمد بن إدريس الشافعي. *الرسالة*. تحقيق أحمد محمد شاكر. بيروت بدون تأريخ.

الشريف المرتضى، الانتصار

الشريف المرتضي علي بن الحسين. *الانتصار*. تحقيق مؤسسة النشر الإسلامي. قم ١٤١٥ هجري قمري.

الشيخ الصدوق، الأمالي

محمد بن علي بن الحسين بن بابويه القمي. تحقيق قسم الدراسات الإسلامية، مؤسسة البعثة. قم ١٤١٧ هجري قمري.

الشيخ الصدوق، الفقيه

محمد بن علي بن الحسين بن بابويه القمي. *من لا يحضره الفقيه*. تحقيق علي أكبر الغفاري. قم بدون تأريخ.

الشيخ الصدوق، معاني الأخبار

محمد بن علي بن الحسين بن بابويه القمي. *معاني الأخبار*. عني بتصحيحه علي أكبر الغفاري. قم ١٣٦١ هجري شمسي.

الطبراني، المعجم الأوسط

سليمان بن أحمد الطبراني. *المعجم الأوسط*. تحقيق طارق بن عوض الله وعبد الحسن بن إبراهيم، مكة ١٩٩٥.

الطبراني، المعجم الكبير

سليمان بن أحمد الطبراني. *المعجم الكبير*. تحقيق حمدي عبد المجيد السلفي. بيروت بدون تأريخ.

الطبري، جامع البيان

محمد بن جرير الطبري. *جامع البيان عن تأويل آي القرآن*. ضبط وتوثيق وتخريج صدقي جميل العطار. بيروت ١٩٩٥.

الطوسي، الاستبصار

محمد بن الحسن بن علي الطوسي. *الاستبصار فيما اختلف من الأخبار*. تحقيق حسن الموسوي الخرسان. طهران ١٣٩٠ هجري قمري.

الطوسي، تهذيب الأحكام

محمد بن الحسن بن علي الطوسي. *تهذيب الأحكام في شرح المقنعة للشيخ المفيد*. تحقيق حسن الموسوي الخرسان. ١٣٩٠ هجري قمري.

الطوسي، الخلاف
محمد بن الحسن بن علي الطوسي. *الخلاف*. تحقيق جماعة من المحققين. قم ١٤٠٧هـ.

الطوسي، المبسوط
محمد بن الحسن بن علي الطوسي. *المبسوط في فقه الإمامية*. تحقيق محمد تقي الكشفي. طهران ١٣٨٧ هـ.

عبد الرزاق، المصنف
عبد الرزاق بن همام الصنعاني. *المصنف*. تحقيق حبيب الرحمان الأعظمي. بيروت ١٩٨٣.

القاضي النعمان، الإقتصار
القاضي النعمان بن محمد. *كتاب الإقتصار*. تحقيق محمد وحيد ميرزا. دمشق ١٩٥٧.

القاضي النعمان، دعائم الإسلام
القاضي النعمان بن محمد. *دعائم الإسلام وذكر الحلال والحرام والقضايا والأحكام عن أهل بيت رسول الله عليه وعليهم أفضل السلام*. تحقيق آصف بن علي أصغر فيضي، القاهرة ١٩٦٣.

القاضي النعمان، شرح الأخبار
القاضي النعمان بن محمد. *شرح الأخبار في فضائل الأئمة الأطهار*. تحقيق محمد الحسيني. قم ١٤١٤ هـ.

القمي، تفسير
علي بن إبراهيم القمي. *تفسير القمي*. تصحيح وتعليق وتقديم طيب الموسوي الجزائري. قم ١٤٠٤ هـ.

الكليني، الكافي
محمد بن يعقوب بن إسحاق الكليني. *الكافي*. تحقيق علي أكبر الغفاري، طهران ١٣٨٨ هـ.

مالك بن أنس، المدونة الكبرى
مالك بن أنس. *المدونة الكبرى برواية سحنون*. بيروت بدون تأريخ.

مالك بن أنس، الموطأ

مالك بن أنس. *الموطأ*. تحقيق محمد فؤاد عبد الباقي. بيروت ١٩٥٨.

المتقي الهندي، كنز العمال

علاء الدين علي المتقي الهندي. *كنز العمال في سنن الأقوال والأفعال*. تحقيق بكري الحياني وصفوة السقا. بيروت ١٩٨٩.

المجلسي، بحار الأنوار

محمد باقر المجلسي. *بحار الأنوار الجامعة لدرر أخبار الأئمة الأطهار*. بيروت ١٩٨٣.

مسلم، الصحيح

مسلم بن الحجاج النيسابوري. *صحيح مسلم*. بيروت بدون تأريخ.

النوري، مستدرك الوسائل

حسين النوري الطبرسي. *مستدرك الوسائل ومستنبط المسائل*. تحقيق مؤسسة آل البيت عليهم السلام لأحياء التراث. بيروت ١٩٨٧.

اليعقوبي، تأريخ

احمد بن أبي يعقوب بن جعفر اليعقوبي. *تأريخ اليعقوبي*. بيروت بدون تأريخ.

فهرس الأعلام

رتبنا أسماء الأعلام حسب ورودها في النصّ.